Charles Ferguson

The religion of democracy:

A manual of devotion

Charles Ferguson

The religion of democracy:
A manual of devotion

ISBN/EAN: 9783337717469

Printed in Europe, USA, Canada, Australia, Japan

Cover: Foto ©Lupo / pixelio.de

More available books at **www.hansebooks.com**

THE RELIGION
OF DEMOCRACY

A MANUAL OF DEVOTION.

BY

CHARLES FERGUSON.

F. TENNYSON NEELY,
PUBLISHER.
LONDON. NEW YORK. CHICAGO.

Copyrighted, 1899,
in the
United States
and
Great Britain,
by
F. TENNYSON NEELY.

(All Rights Reserved.)

FORE-WORD:

A SYMBOL.

On the way across the park that stretches its *parterres* between the Capitol and the new Congressional Library, one may stop and rest on a stone bench in front of the vast, pillared, porticoed, Græco-Roman building where Congress meets. Close by is the togaed statue of Washington, seated in a kind of curule chair, and pointing, with one finger, up to heaven. To the right and left, in flawless symmetry, stretch the classic wings of the Capitol, fit each for a Parthenon; and over all, the pompous dome, Argus-eyed with serried little glimmering windows, broods and settles mightily down in obstinate immensity.

Seen thus, in the afternoon sun, the building grows into one's mind as a symbol of things that have been, but are passing away. The suggestions of the scene are reminiscent. This is the America of foreign and ancient tutelage, trailing the Old World; the nation that did not know the originality of its vocation, and did not venture to breathe deep. It is the America of the paper constitution, of orations on the classic model, of moralizing art, and intolerant virtues; the land of Spartan seclusion from the world, yet of huge comfortableness; the land of the perfect plan that must not be spoiled; the

Fore Word.

sophomoric land that had not yet loved and suffered.

Over against this picture there is in my mind a vision of very different suggestion. There are nights when, looking from my window across huddling chimneys and the flat roofs of houses, I see the Capitol transfigured. The colossal dome, white and magnificent in the moonlight, swims in a luminous, electric mist that comes brimming up from the city. The glorious ghost of the Capitol, looming over sordid chimney-tops, seems like a symbol of the new age and the America that is in the making. Here is modernity, the age of electricity—and mystery. Here is the type of the longing of the people, the awe of science, the passion for the eternal, the cosmic fear, the victorious faith, the contradictions of life, the problems, the poverty, the tragic perplexity, the cry in the night; here steel-clad battleships and sudden war, the knight-errantry of the Republic, the pathos of Spain and Italy and Greece and China, immense expansion and contraction, the old ethnic hate, the effacement of boundaries, world-wide equality, fraternity, ecumenic democracy, unanimity.

This shimmering dome in the moonlight, mystic, aerial, portentous, seems a wraith of revolution—the prophetic, insurgent spirit of the nation.

I perceive how deep down in the infinite are the springs of history. And I am reassured of the love of God.

WASHINGTON, 1899.

CONTENTS.

CHAPTER I.
The Return to the Concrete.................... 7

CHAPTER II.
The Man of the Modern Spirit.................. 24

CHAPTER III.
The Revolution Absolute....................... 86

CHAPTER IV.
The Discovery of America...................... 57

CHAPTER V.
The Discount of Glory......................... 70

CHAPTER VI.
The Sovereignty of the People................. 91

CHAPTER VII.
The World of News............................. 110

CHAPTER VIII.
The Caste of Goodness......................... 184

CHAPTER IX.
The Rise of a Democratic Catholic Church...... 145

The Religion of Democracy.

CHAPTER I.

THE RETURN TO THE CONCRETE.

I.—The spirit of the age is saying to its children: Have faith. Make yourself at home. This is your own house. The laws were made for you, gravitation and the chemical affinities, not you for them. No one can put you out of the house. Stand up; the ceiling is high.

This is eternity—now—you are sunk as deep in it, wrapped as close in it as you ever will be. The future is an illusion; it never arrives. It flies before you as you advance. Always it is to-day, and after a long while it is still to-day; and after death and a thousand years, it is to-day. You have great deeds to perform, and you must do them now.

If you should act with simplicity and boldness, do you think that you would have to stand alone and take the consequences? Have you no

The Religion of Democracy.

idea that God would back you up? That is as if you thought this world were mainly bones, and the soul a pale prisoner, looking wistfully through the ribs of it. It is as if God were caught in His own body, and could not move otherwise than according to the laws laid down in the books, and as if all the people that pass in the streets had wan, scared souls caught in their bodies like animals in a trap. For if God may not do as He likes, how can a man be other than a prisoner?

God is free. Go out doors and see for yourself. Are not the trees wayward and whimsical? Is not the wind let loose, and is not the sea savage enough? Do not the birds wheel and turn as they like? So does God do as He likes. He is not caught in His body; neither are you. You can move if you try; have faith. Have faith in God.

I come to you with great ideas, ideas big with revolution—but they are common. You will recognize them as your own. Only it is necessary to put words to them. Words are the wings of ideas; without words they brood, but cannot fly. And these ideas of ours must fly from land to land and kindle the whole earth.

Civilization grows senile; but the soul is always young. Witness stoutly for the soul, and you shall renew the youth of the world.

II.—Are you grieved to see a crowd of people met together to worship God, but not frankly believing in God, and not daring to risk their lives upon the moral law? Do you dislike to see a crowd of bankers and business men met together to worship Money, but not frankly believing in the power of money or daring to trust their souls to it? Does it pain you to hear them talk of good faith and honor and the morals of the country? Do you long to see men simple of heart and honest, believing flatly in the soul, or in the five senses, without dodging or subterfuge? Come, then, it shall be so. Stop here and resolve that you will not compromise any more.

It is not so bad to be a materialist. If you keep to the facts you will not get away from God. The moral laws are not separate from matter. They are wrought into the fiber of the material world. You cannot dig anywhere without striking them.

III.—The desire and passion of God is to beget souls of men through the long-birth processes and the eons of nature; souls that shall

The Religion of Democracy.

be separate from His own soul, and that shall stand over against Him, so that He can look upon them, and have communion with them and be not Alone. And in order that the souls of men shall become thus separate and distinct from the soul of God, it is necessary that God should hide Himself, and that men should learn to trust their own thoughts and their own eyes. In this withdrawal of God is the peril and crisis of creation, the inevitable opportunity of sin, the tragedy and pathos of our life upon this earth.

Do you not understand the taciturnity of God? Do you not see why it is that He does not blazon His name in the sky, or accost you with words—why He bosoms you in His arms, and turns His face away, and waits, and is patient and silent? Have you had dreams of Nirvana and sickly visions and raptures? Have you imagined that the end of your life is to be absorbed back into the life of God, and to flee the earth and forget all? Or do you want to walk on air or fly on wings, or build a heavenly city in the clouds? Come, let us take our kit on our shoulders, and go out and build the city *here*.

IV.—You need not doubt that the embryo of

The Religion of Democracy.

the soul of man is to be found in the plants and animals.

Environment is the body of God, and the germinal soul of man is lapped in God like a child in the womb. The desire and longing of God is to get the soul born; and there is a labor of eons in the parturition.

God could not make a free soul out of hand. He could not make it at all. The soul must claim its own liberty and life.

And so one must say that the free spirit of man is uncreated, is not made by God, but begotten of Him. Words fail, for you touch here the hem of the robe of the eternal mystery. But it is not to be wondered at that God should suffer so long to integrate a soul out of His own soul—a soul that should look Him in the face and be faithful to Him.

V.—Environment is not everything: life has had a will of its own from the beginning. The living thing is pressed up close against the life of God. God is free and omnific, except that He cannot compel what is his heart's desire— that the creature shall act from within itself. He cannot require that it shall have faith.

The living thing is free, but weak and faint of heart; and with great difficulty it learns to

The Religion of Democracy.

believe and strive. Mystery of the love of God, and the infinite patience and tenderness! Like a baby's fingers feeling vaguely over the breasts of a woman, and like the thrill and response and the tightening clasp, so does God answer back every vague and timid adventure of faith! And this they call Natural Selection.

How perverse and pathetic the desires of the animals. But they all get what they ask for —long necks and trunks, flapping ears and branching horns and corrugated hides—anything, if only they will believe in life and try.

What imaginable caricature has not God submitted to in order that a man might be born in His image—and a beautiful woman!

VI.—Civilizations are destroyed by great ideas, apprehended, but not lived up to.

Philosophy, poetry, science, art and the mysteries of religion are forever beckoning men on to a more intimate contact with God and with the interior and elemental world. If men would think, and dig, and pray, and paint and carve with a perfect daring, all would be well and they would have built the Holy City long ago. But they have not faith enough: they recoil from the shock and risk, touch the deeper mysteries and shrink back. They become sen-

The Religion of Democracy.

timental about God and separate the sacred from the secular. They refuse the desire of the heart and breed in their bodies a swarm of petty appetites, divisive and corrupting. The force of the divine and elemental passion in them goes to the refinement of prurient arts. And the corruption of the best is the worst corruption.

The death of nations is in the rejection of their own most wistful desire. The Truth appears, is seen, touched, handled, and debated, is accepted notionally, but rejected in fact, and crucified.

Europe and America to-day are sick with the nightmare of their dreams. They have dreamed of Democracy, and in their dreams have achieved liberty—but only in their dreams, not otherwise.

The madhouses are full of people that breathe in the real world, but live in their ideals. And the nations are mad with this madness, and are ready to kill the Lord of Life.

With God the thought and the act are one. The worlds are sustained in their courses, the storm rages, the birds sing, and your heart is beating because God is thinking.

But we see that the world is full of sentimentalists. The courts, the academies and the cham-

The Religion of Democracy.

bers of commerce are mostly ruled by absent-minded people who say and do not, and know not what they do.

The Devil's right name is abstraction. To lie and to know it is to evince that one is not altogether a liar; but to lie and not to know it is to be false indeed. This is Sin, and the end of it is death. But death is better than sin. It must be better than sin, because it is nearer the truth.

VII.—These wretched fellows that scramble so breathlessly for a competency, and cannot hold up their heads if their coats are rough—*Les miserables!* Have pity.

And these others that are seeking a fabulous chimera—what they call millions—with sharp, metallic speech like the click of a telegraph, who think in numbers only and cabalistic signs and counters; who give each other winks and tips—men that know everything and nothing, that can predict eclipses and cause them, make famines with a turn of the wrist, without meaning any harm; these fantastical triflers, fooling with their punk in the powder magazine—certainly they hold their place by a slight and precarious tenure. They scarcely touch the facts of God's earth with the tips of their toes, and they are as little indigenous here as shining

The Religion of Democracy.

angels with wings. Their ignorance of values is profound. They know not how much blood goes into things. And they are practical men in the same sense as the old card-cronies that sit and play in the back rooms of the saloon behind the green baize screens. They know the rules of the games that they have spun like spiders out of their own bodies, and they can play to win without troubling to think.

The business interests of the country—mysterious, intangible thing! Do the business interests require that people shall be fed and clothed and housed? And does the doing of business mean that things worth doing shall get done somehow? No; only that there shall be bustle and running to and fro, with infinite complication of accounts, and in the end that somebody shall—make money! Golden cloudland and most delicate moonshine! Oh, practical men!

VIII.—And has any one yet seen a cultivated man or made the acquaintance of a man of the world? Certainly not among the pampered or the privileged. These read all the poems of the ages, and skim through all the sacred books, but do not understand one line; flit restlessly from town to country and circumnavigate the globe, yet never see a sunrise or meet a man!

The Religion of Democracy.

How can one who lives without thanks upon the labor of others, who has been dandled all his life in the strong arms of the laborers so that his feet have never for a moment felt the drastic earth, who has never wrestled naked with God for a blessing, or felt a common elemental need—how can such an one know anything of the omens of history, how judge rightly and decide what is human and of immortal value in books and pictures, or what is just in laws? How can he fight the battles of the weak, or answer the questions of the simple; interpret the meaning of the prophets, or comprehend the passion of Christ?

Did any one suppose that he could get the humanities and leave out mankind?

This aristocracy of culture, this pomp and foolery of *bibelots*, must seem to the strong, battling saints and scripture-makers that look down upon it, like a masquerade of footmen, a kind of high life below stairs. Is it not known that books are sacrificial, that they must be lived and suffered before they are written, and lived and suffered before they are read?

Is not a poem an enterprise and an act of faith? And are these fireside story-tellers, these table-talkers and ramblers in the woods—poets? Do they put words to what you mean to do? Are

The Religion of Democracy.

they the makers of new cities and new eras? Are they the spokesmen of the laborers? Do you think they know what Democracy means? Can they put into speech the dumb, passionate longing of the people? Can they face a mob without flinching—the mob of moneyed men and men of fashion and men of letters—and the madness of the people?

IX.—If you pass by the least considerable man, you pass by all the humanities and the divinities, and set your heart on what is transient and cheap. There is a wide ocean of difference between taking in the last man and leaving him out. It is not a question of one man, but of humanity. If you leave anybody out, you must leave your own soul out, and must live thenceforth by the butler's standard. It is a fearful thing to belong to the exclusive circles.

Every interest that does not directly relate to the soul is an abstraction. The soul is the concrete absolute. This is the soul's world clear through, and the inmost law of it is the law of the relation of persons. And to deal with material objects or with ideas without reference to persons, is to invert the order of the universe and to take things altogether as they are not.

The Religion of Democracy.

Do you suppose that God cares anything for His performances except as they relate to persons? Do you suppose that He is vain of the shimmering sea or the tints of the evening sky? Do you not understand that Life rules here, and that everything exists for Life? The sun does not make signs to the moon, and the stars do not beckon one another; but everything beckons the living soul. It is a shame, then, to dodge and defer to things or to your own achievements or to any man's. It is a shame to take circuitous courses or to desire social consideration and influence as a means of accomplishing one's ends—as if one were a stranger and an alien here, picking his way fearfully through an enemy's country and compelled to make the most of a scanty equipment.

You need not be afraid, any more than a duck is afraid of drowning or a bird of falling. In your inmost soul you are as well suited to the whole cosmical order and every part of it as to your own body. You belong here. Did you suppose that you belonged to some other world than this, or that you belonged nowhere at all—were just a waif on the bosom of the eternities? Is not that unthinkable? Incontestably you belong here. Have not the biologists told you all about it? Nothing is plainer than that God has been at measureless pains that you should suit your surroundings, and that your surroundings should suit you with a perfect correspondence at every point. Conceivably He might have flung you into a world that was unrelated to you, and might have left you to be acclimated at your own risk; but you happen to know that this is not the case. You have lived here always; this is the ancestral demesne; for ages and ages you have looked out of these same windows upon the celestial landscape and the star-deeps. You are at home.

X.—If there is any cosmical ordinance that you do not like, then there is something wrong with you. If there is any necessary thing that you shrink from—as death, or labor, or growth and long waiting—then you are not well and sound. To draw back from a fact is to prefer a lie.

If you say you do not like the contact of the earth, or the contact of the people, and would withdraw yourself from them, then there is nothing left for you but to live in a world of phantoms and shadows. A hundred million men, possessed of the same illusions, can agree to reject death, and labor and love, and to pass their days as if these things did not exist, or

The Religion of Democracy.

were altogether alien; they can agree upon arbitrary signs and can regard as great and weighty the things of their own imagination and the passing fashions—but they are dreamers, and the facts remain to be reckoned with at last.

The cosmos is sound all through, absolutely valid; and it covers the whole ground. There is no room for another universe. If you do not like this one, the door is open into the inane.

In the old Hebrew story, Adam would not dress and keep the garden, and so get wise in the divine and vital way by daily contact with real things, but would eat wisdom and ruminate upon it. The original sin was the rejection of the real world and a flight to dreamland; and the healing penalty was a hard necessity that should draw back the man and the woman to the firm, resistant earth—labor, in bread-getting and in child-bearing.

All the failures of the world have come from this flinching from the keen and open air—the attempt to escape into a made-up world within fences and behind doors. The failure of history is in egotism, and this is egotism—to consider oneself as having no essential relationships, no rootage in the real world.

The Religion of Democracy.

XI.—Does there rise before you the vision of the long-drawn misery and terror of the world, the tyrannies and blasphemies, the collapses, the mere dull cycles and aimless, rotary motion? Do you feel yourself environed to-day by a vast and intricate fabric of make-believes, and things-agreed-upon—religions, politics, and social customs that do not take account of God and the soul; charitable institutions contrived as makeshifts to avoid the insistent obligation of the moral law, riches that are afraid of their own shadow, and poverty that is afraid of riches; art that is at war with nature; and science that spies and pries in the forms and phenomena of things, but falters at the primal, living fact?

Do you discern the cause of the contradiction between what is right and what seems to be expedient? On one hand is the real and elemental world, with its eternal perspectives, its insistent and tender intimacies with your inner heart, commanding your trust and obedience, your consecration to the aim of God in the fulfillment of the destiny of mankind; and on the other hand is the sham world fabricated with immense labor, a hundred times destroyed by the inrush of the elements, and a hundred times reconstituted by the conceit and fear of men—

The Religion of Democracy.

an asylum of escape from nature, and truth, and the strong compulsions of love and duty, a castle of compromise, wherein there is no right and no wrong, but only a shifting expediency and escape from conclusions; wherein religion is made a question of credulity and of being baptized, and the only object of devotion that is offered to the soul is comfort, money, and to be well thought of.

Of these two worlds, it is the latter—the world of compromises—that is nearest at hand and most in evidence. It surrounds you and inmeshes you. If you start to do anything in a straightforward and natural way, it constrains and embarrasses you. You are made to feel that your deepest instincts are not to be trusted, that senility is wiser than youth, that the roundabout way is shortest to your aim, and that as between right and wrong, the truth and a lie, a middle course is always best. The business of living becomes a delicate art of balancing, everything is at last a question of expert testimony and statistics; there is no sure good or sure evil until after all the committees have reported; meanwhile, your affair is to be as comfortable as you can. This is the world that environs you and holds you close in its intricate tissue of expediencies. Over beyond

The Religion of Democracy.

is the world of the elemental moral forces, the divine passions and devotions, the world where the artists work free, and daring, and youth is sure and swift to its aim. And between your world of prudent hypocrisies and that passionate, real world, there is a valley of shadows and dreadful doubts.

Do you not see that there is need of but just one thing, and that that one thing is—faith?

Have faith, then. Come, take the risks. It is time to go through the valley and try what is beyond.

CHAPTER II.

THE MAN OF THE MODERN SPIRIT.

I.—THE greatness of the modern spirit is its humility. It keeps close to the puissant ground; it will walk in the real world. Do not be deceived by the brag and flourish; the heart of the age is humble. And it is only by humility that you can enter into its meaning, utter its longing, or fulfill its faith.

The modern spirit is a tall, fair woman, standing at her door expecting to see the Lord of Heaven and Earth pass by in the dusty road and get a message from Him. Or shall we say that it is a strong man, horsed and riding through the world, challenging all pleasant lies and vain pretensions, seeking a sacred fact even in the face of despair, and as he rides, crying: "Truth, the truth; though it slay me, yet will I trust it." Or, again, it is, if you like, a laborer, crowned, or a king in gray clothes, toiling.

The quintessence of the modern spirit is faith

in the incarnation. The faith that has gone out from the pulpits and the pews is walking abroad in the streets. Parsons and priests, synods and sacred councils, may not be half so sure that the Son of God must needs be brought up in Nazareth as the workers and fighters are, and the plain people that pass by. Do you know why this name of Jesus pursues you; why you cannot turn and look over your shoulder without seeing Him, or something that reminds you of Him? It is because He is the man of the modern spirit.

He does not talk in abstractions; He is concrete, practical, personal. He rests on what He is—rests on the facts and their self-vindicating power. He makes no boasts and no excuses. He is like nature; there is in Him the calm of nature and its violence; the passion of nature and its incompleteness and progress. He has nature's grand silences; He waits sublimely. He keeps close to the earth, the ground is always under His feet. A sea or a mountain cannot put Him out or make Him little. He speaks with authority because He is at home in the world; He rises from the dead because He is on good terms with death. The age is dawning that shall understand these things; it is the mission of the modern spirit to explain them.

The Religion of Democracy.

The message of Jesus is moral adventure; go on, take the risk; commit yourself confidently to the eternal currents and the natural order.

He takes in the unity of the cosmos, and is tranquilly confident of the validity of its laws. He is determined to get at the facts; He shrinks from nothing, not from disease, or the sweat and grime. He is sure of the inexhaustible resources of health and of the forgiveness of sins. He never compromises because He is close to His facts, and they do not compromise. He moves straight to His conclusion with an inflexible logic. He demonstrates the axioms of the concrete; He does not argue; He illustrates. His is the absolute science and the consummate art and enterprise. He is the pioneer of a new world, and the Man of Destiny. He comprehends Europe, America and the future. He knows what is bound up in Democracy. He radiates courage and power, and to believe in Him is to have faith.

II.—Shall one suppose that God regards a subject from all sides and in every possible light before He decides what to do, or that He attends specifically and separately to every motion that comes from the brain of an ant, or the wing of a fly? Is it not plain that the universe is governed by vital impulses; that millions and millions of consequences flow from the whir of a fly's wing, and that its footfall shakes the firmament? Most likely God does not attend to the consequences; He attends to the life of the fly.

You lift your finger and stir every atom in Sirius and Orion; and so every living thing occupies the whole universe, and has something to do with every mass and every motion. How all the lines cross and recross in an infinite maze! What a weltering palimpsest is the world of phenomena! No man ever read a word of it except he had the key of it all in his own soul.

Behind mass and motion is might, and back of might is mind; and the beginning of science is in congeniality with God.

The larger word for science is conscience. And the final test of the authenticity and permanence of a physical fact is its moral reasonableness—its congruity with right. Do you protest sometimes with vehemence that God is cruel and unjust? Justice must then be rooted very deep in the heart of things, since it dares to confront omnipotence with a fist so feeble to back its claim! But you say well; you must

The Religion of Democracy.

not submit to be bullied by earthquakes and tornadoes, or by the sun, moon and stars. If royalties, and usuries, and monopolies are unjust, they must not be tolerated; and if gravitation and cohesion are unjust, they must be put down.

III.—Unless you believe in the reasonableness of the world it is idle to think about it at all. And if you should spend your life in plotting to escape what is inevitable or in denying the plain ordinances of human kinship, then you would be derationalized; and science would become impossible to you. If one is unloving and a coward, it is impossible that he should know anything; there is no use in having brains without faith and courage.

A man cannot stand aside and learn the laws of this whirring, dangerous world by holding out his brains at arm's length; his frail body must go with his brains into the midst of the *mêlée*. You cannot learn any more than you now know without venturing something that you have not tried. Did any one suppose that, sitting at ease in his study chair, cushioned and walled in, he could draw knowledge out of printed books? It is impossible. And Holy Scripture, when the devil reads it, is devilish.

The Religion of Democracy.

For a long while we have been under the spell of those men of science that have fancied that they could separate their minds from themselves, have supposed that they could set their brains working in the midst of things, while themselves standing aloof, disengaged and *nonchalant*, waiting for results. They have sent forth the fabulous instrument of knowledge as far as possible from the center of the warm and vital sphere of human feeling, and have set it down on the frontiers of consciousness, where humanity is reduced to its lowest terms almost is not humanity. If they could wholly outside of consciousness they would have done it; but they could not. So they have put up with so much of feeling as goes to the perception that things are bulky and that they move. It is not much of a perception; probably worms can perceive that much. Starting thus, the aim of these absent-minded *savants* has been to work their machine of knowledge back to themselves, taking notes by the way, automatic, mechanical, exact. They have tried to explain themselves by something as nearly as possible foreign to themselves, to construe love and rage and hunger in terms of mass and motion. It is prodigious gymnastics, but it will have to be given up.

The Religion of Democrıcy.

And yet this thing which has been called the method of science is not wholly perverse. It has a history and a *rationale,* an excuse—even a kind of justification. So long had men looked out upon the world with mere greed and fear, so long had they looked through eyes blinded with passion and seen only the reflection of their own superstition and lust, so long been confounded by the irrefragible fact, which never would wait upon their wishes; it was natural and inevitable that science should turn ascetic and pharisaic, that it should mortify and flagellate every human feeling, should resolve to be only eye—as the monks of the desert resolved to be only soul—that it should reject the cosmic gospel, worship the law, and crucify the Son of Man. It was a bitter error and failure, but it was natural enough.

So, then, both the old knowledge roads turn out to be blind alleys. One we have already decided to abandon, and the other we shall soon give up. Not if we know it do we travel now the old blundering road of rapturous superstition and conceit, expecting the laws of the universe to budge and conform whenever we cry or clap our hands. Our disillusioned *savants* have fixed their *no-thoroughfare* at the hither end of that byway, and so have done us a service. But the road that they have led us into is bad with another kind of badness; and there is a blank wall at the end of it, with a death's-head on it for a sign. That road, too, we shall abandon, and turn back with shuddering fear. The haughty high priests of science may rend their gaberdines and cry their law; but we will not listen, for by their law we die. And the emaciated scientific monks may preach from their pillars their stifling clinic gospel till they drop, but they cannot stay us. The heart of the age is hungering against them for love and liberty; for health and the tonic air.

IV.—The way of valid science is the way of the modern spirit. It begins with an act of faith—an immense assumption—to wit, that the whole world is constitutionally at one with itself; that it is a universe; that it has no alien elements, no unassimilable fate, no intrinsic contradictions. This assumption is the great adventure of the age. We are committing ourselves to it without calculating the consequences. It distinguishes this age from all other ages as, *par excellence*, the age of faith.

There is nowhere in Europe or America today an accepted philosophy that can be called

The Religion of Democracy.

skeptical in the ancient sense of that word. Nobody denies now the possibility of knowledge; nobody draws a crowd now to the teaching that the world is, for practical purposes, unknowable. The nearest approach to old-time skepticism is made by the straight sect of orthodox theologians. For to teach, as they do, that the most useful and important knowledge can neither be got nor proved by contact of living men with the present world, but must be handed down from some luminous spot in the past and received by authority—this is pretty nearly Pyrrhonism: it is Pyrrhonism plus a miracle or two.

The vast majority of our contemporaries, now in the dawn of the twentieth century, for the first time in history are ready to assume somewhat recklessly and airily for the most part, as not counting the cost, but in good faith, too, that the whole world is reasonable, that it hangs together to the minutest detail, and that there are no gaps or *crevasses* in it to swallow up the mind. This assumption is made in the face of death, disease, the antagonism of national and private interests and the sum total of adverse experience. It is a magnificent risk; probably most of us would shrink from it if we should measure the height and depth of it.

The Religion of Democracy.

Nay, do we not all shrink and falter and deny the spirit of the age? The first comer will tell you that in his view death and labor are a disadvantage, and that his interest and yours are at variance.

But if death is a disdvantage, and yet is inevitable, how then can the world be reasonable? And if your interest is opposed to your neighbor's, what becomes of the congruity of things and the unity of the world? If that is good for him which is bad for you, then there are at least two universes—yours and his; and two gods, or else there is confusion and no God.

V.—You cannot understand what God does unless you are of the same stuff as God. Shall the clay say to the potter: What doest thou? Can things be understood by a thing? Must not the creature pass over to the status of the Creator before it can understand anything of the creation? Can a *savant* be other than a savior? Does any one suppose that a man that feels that he is transient and is afraid of death, can make contributions to science, or that that which flows with the stream can measure its force or survey it?

It is a vast pretension, but doubtless it is the will of God that it should be made. The chil-

The Religion of Democracy.

dren of the spirit of the age are passing the timid and halting creeds, and professing their confidence in the possibility of science. Mystics! Transcendentalists! They will believe what they cannot prove, if only it is reasonable, and they will deny what seems most obvious, if it is absurd.

It is announced that it is not necessary to clutch at the face of nature for a living; that we are here to stay, and that there is harm, not in hunger or death, but only in that which is inhuman.

They do not offer proofs that pain is powerless, that it is expedient to be just, or that the soul is immortal. But they accept the witness of the spirit of the age that God is reasonable, and that we can get rid of our unreasonableness and can understand His meaning. Pain, then, will be to us what it is to Him; justice will be as good for us as it is for Him, and we shall not die unless He dies, nor be imprisoned unless He is arrested. The spirit comes with no credentials that can be weighed in the higgling scale of culture; there are no certificates or statistics. Confessedly this is a jangling world for one bent on quick pleasures, but there may be rhythm and music in it for a lover who can wait.

The Religion of Democracy.

The propositions of the spirit are not on trial, but the world is on trial. The sunset of the age is full of flaming portents. So it was at the end of the eighteenth, and at the beginniug of the nineteenth century. They set up then on the altar of the Church of Our Lady in Paris a kind of hoyden Goddess of Reason—striking symbol of a science that rejected the generous risks of faith, and would make sure of its pastimes. The portents were then fulfilled, and the science that would risk nothing lost everything—lost its senses at last, and went stark mad. It shall not be so again if it can be helped. There may be blood and tears, but not like that. It is necessary to deal more magnanimously with God, and take the risks.

CHAPTER III.

THE REVOLUTION ABSOLUTE.

I.—DEMOCRACY implies infinity. Men are declared to be equal because it is discovered that all men, the least as well as the greatest, have or may have access to the Infinite. The obvious disparities become insignificant, in view of this great commonness. Infinity plus a million is seen to be no more than infinity plus one. If it were not for religion democracy would be inconceivable; if a man's soul is measurable and transient, democracy is ridiculous.

II.—At the heart of life there is a primal contradiction. That is why the deepest sayings have the form of paradox—as that a man must die to live; must lose his life to find it.
To resolve this antinomy is to resolve all antinomies; it lies back of all and comprehends all. It is the Sphinx riddle of the ages, and it gives to life its tragic perplexity. It is the

The Religion of Democracy.

burden and passion of the social struggle upon which we are entering. Never before was the question proposed so squarely and inevitably; never before did the world-issue translate itself into historic terms so concrete and practical. That is why this period is the most signal and momentous of all historic epochs. The revolution that is impending is not relative and provisional; it is the revolution absolute.

The world riddle may be come at in three principal ways: to wit, as cosmical—comprehending the whole world process; as historical—having relation to the narrower horizon of human history; and as personal, relating to the issues of the individual life.

Regarding the cosmical process, we see, to speak according to the books, the mechanical passing into the chemical, chemical into vital, vital into psychic, and psychic into spiritual. The divisions are arbitrary and school-made, and they have served to complicate the simple principle that is involved. The process has been called evolution: it may be that, but it is more; it is revolution. It is characteristically, not only a development, but a conversion; not only a progression, but a right-about-face. The object becomes subject; the thing made becomes maker; the clay becomes potter.

The Religion of Democracy.

III.—Regard the historic drama. History begins with the birth of the idea of liberty; what went before was prehistoric, dim, undifferentiated, protoplasmic. The primeval tribe and village commune, brooding under the unchallenged sway of habit and tradition, are cast for no rôle in the historic drama. Theirs is the prologue of the play, serving only to indicate the point from which the story runs. History begins when the hard cake of custom is shattered by ambition and the will-to-live. The action is dual, has two principal phases; and these stand in sharp contrast and contradiction. History is ancient and modern.

The ancient spirit had free course until this era; it maintains a prevailing influence to this day. The modern spirit proceeds from the Man of Nazareth; it grapples with the other in irreducible antagonism. Both strive for liberty; but the liberty of one is in self-assertion, of the other in self-abandonment. One has pride, authority, ambition, circumspection; the other, humor, veracity, enterprise, insight. One finds its characteristic expression in philosophy, the other in science. The master of all ancient society—and of modern society only in its failure and reaction—is the self-made man—or, if you please, the cultivated man—the man intent

The Religion of Democracy.

upon the process of his own making. The idea that life is fulfilled through studied effort to make the most of oneself was the idea of Cato as well as Caiaphas. Pericles and Plato, Seneca and Cicero, all gave their best energies to self-improvement—if not to material advancement, then to intellectual and spiritual culture. They were all self-made men. There is the pomp and pretentiousness, the artificiality and rejection of nature's flowing grace. And there is about them all a touch of that self-conciousness that belongs to men that have made themselves and are disposed to admire the performance—a certain lack of humor, or, if you please, of humility. The notion that the creations of antique art are representative of the tone and color of antique living is one of the great historical illusions; they were but wistfully reminiscent of a fancied golden age that had passed away. Great Pan was dead, and the sweet divinities had fled from wood and stream before the dawn of history. When the self-made man came into the world, the gods of nature gave up and left.

The gayety of nature is a gift that the modern spirit has in store; for characteristically the modern man is not proud, but keeps to the ground. He cares not much for what is called culture, feeling that it is somehow vitally ab-

The Religion of Democracy.

surd that a man should fix his eyes on his own spiritual processes or spend his time in improving his own mind or his own soul. The modern man cares for science and reverences a fact, keeps close to the real world and gives himself to his work. His concern is with things external to himself, and he counts himself successful as he becomes participant in the ordinary business of the universe. The man of the ancient spirit fled from the common people; the modern man turns back to the laborers and the poor.

In a word, the typical man of the old order feels himself caught and confounded in the creation, and his freedom is to get out to the Creator; while the typical man of the new order feels himself identified with the Creator, and his freedom is, like God's, to get into the creation.

The historic drama thus reveals the same contradiction that we encounter on the wider stage of the cosmos. The innumerable contradictions of history are resolvable into one primal contradiction. The object becomes subject; man passes from the status of the creature to that of the creator. The old order is not improved, but is dissolved by its antithesis. History is not only evolutionary, but revolution-

The Religion of Democracy.

IV.—We discern the same principle again when we look to the issues of life in the individual. The typical man is a microcosm and he resumes in his own experience the history of the race. His life is a revolution. At first he broods and is silent; he is protoplasmic, tribal, passive. He rises thence to the passion for liberty—feeling the encumbrance and constraint of the creation. He tries to escape into the ideal—becomes an ambitious dreamer, a philosopher, and politician, and breaks with his kin to dispute with the doctors. With the refinement of his will he is more subtly beset with the longing for power and prodigy and glory, and these things possess him for a time. But to the strophe succeeds the antistrophe. In the crisis of his life he puts behind him all the things that had been set before him, and faces the other way. Thenceforward his interest is not what may become of him, but what may the creation become, and he sets his face steadfastly toward Jerusalem. He is no longer creature, but creator; not made, but begotten; not the child of heredity fatality and circumstance, but the Son of God. This was the beginning of modernity.

V.—Democracy stands to-day at the grand

The Religion of Democracy.

junction and crossroads of history. The world-antinomy now announces itself in unescapable contradictions. The old order and the self-made man have now at length to reckon with the new order and the man of the modern spirit. We can postpone the issue no longer. Democracy now at length, the world over, takes in the last man; and that is fatal to the old way of the world. For the last man is a million—the hitherto bulked, estimated multitude. It was something that the masses should get themselves enumerated, and should become a multitude. But that is nothing to what is in store; the counters are going to take a hand in the play.

This is the very whirlwind of moral revolution. The world has never seen anything like it up to this date. Always, heretofore, revolutions have meant merely some wider distribution of privilege, more top hats and togas, and that ten thousand instead of ten should mulct the multitude. But now at length it has been decided that the multitude should not be mulcted any more; and this resolution, adhered to, will turn the world around and set the foundations of society on new and hitherto undiscovered bases.

The bottom fact of social philosophy, ranging wide through literature, the amenities and

The Religion of Democracy.

courtesies, religion and the fine arts, is an economic fact. The books and pictures, the etiquettes and rituals, are what they are, according to the terms of the settlement of the bread question. And this, not because flesh is God, but because God is flesh.

Now the broadest, the basic fact of the old world which democracy comes to destroy, is that it has got its bread with injustice. The old world has been, by the witness of all the wise, a vain world and a liar, a world of dreams and inveterate illusions. And the spring and source of all its lies is theft. Speculative mistakes in the theory of morals may be got along with; it is the practical lie that kills. And theft is the root of all abstraction—the very substance of vanity, the stuff that dreams are made of.

Always one class has preyed upon another class. The strong, from the beginning, have stolen their bread; and, what is worse, they have despised their bakers. They have discredited the natural facts of alimentation, and they have sponged upon the poor. What hope of wise, deliberate science, of joyous, perennial art and permanent civic glory in a world that is ashamed of its stomach, filches its food, and despises the souls of laborers? What hope of

The Religion of Democracy.

religion if you flout the central sacrament of the body of God?

To be sure, there has always been a man that would not lie—an artist, a poet; there have been true books and pictures, and perfect deeds, an unbroken tradition and prophecy of democracy. Nobody ever wrote, ruled, carved or painted, and left any one out, without leaving himself out, and being forgotten. The torch has been carried on, but flickering, like a candle in a cave. And the prophecy is still waiting its fulfillment.

Do you wonder that the fine arts are overfine or underfine; that their beauty is wistful; that the literatures lapse and die, and the great scriptures of the world, given for joy, sound in our ears only of judgment; that history swirls in dizzy, bewildering cycles; that science is full of panic and terror, and philosophy is only a wan surmise? It is to be written on the sepulchers of the old cities: They took the bread of the poor, and they despised the souls of the laborers.

VI.—Yet remember this contempt for the poor is not the imperfection, the flaw in the old social systems that are passing. It is their principle, and *sine qua non*. The flaw is the suspicion of an infinite soul, a qualm of the sense of eternity. So long as contempt for the poor is steadfast and consistent, it furnishes an entirely practicable ground of social stability. It bases and sanctions a social arrangement that is satisfactory to the strong—to those able to maintain it—and unsatisfactory only to the weak, who are unable to overthrow it. On the one side, the gains are allied to force; and on the other, loss goes hand in hand with disability. That is a workable arrangement; left to itself it might endure a million years. But it has not been left to itself. There has come into the world a great power of revolution. Contempt of the poor has been abashed in a great presence—the presence of a poor man—a laborer and a victim. The awe of suffering, defeat, death—that is the destroyer of the aristocratic *régime*. The man of the people is the man of sorrows.

VII.—The man willing to die becomes the master of the world. This is an overture of universal emancipation; it excludes no one. The beginning of liberty is the discovery of the beautifulness and the infinite succor of death. There can be no freedom among men who are afraid to die; and a people to whom

The Religion of Democracy.

success is necessary cannot build a city that is great. The cities of the world, New York, London, Paris, are provincial; we have yet to build a metropolis—a city of the soul, a city whose citizens are not afraid of death—a capital of democracy. Death is the revealer of the soul; therefore death is the great democrat.

VIII.—The soul is infinite, and it cannot rest until it rests in the infinite. But lust and hunger are not infinite, and neither are the titillations of pleasure and praise. And the agony or hope of unescapable death—of involuntary dying—these one can measure. But there is something in death itself and in the master of death that you cannot measure. There is no infinity in just dying; but to see a man that is willing to die for love, that goes to meet death in the way, that makes a boast of pain, and, with perfect sweetness and sanity, celebrates defeat—that is to be witness of the palpable infinite. It is like an arrow passing swiftly up into the air and not returning; like the still energy of planets or the resistless growing of the grass, or like the haunting, thrilling murmur of remembered music that faded down the avenue as the soldiers went to war. You are left endlessly expectant; you cannot come to an

The Religion of Democracy.

end, but must follow that which is beyond, and still beyond.

This is greatness. In this immensity the soul comes to its own and finds what is good and satisfactory. It is this that is intended by the repose in action, the poised energy of great art.

It remains with you and consoles. After the money-lord has passed by, clinking his gold, and the war-lord, clanking his steel, this stays, and is sufficiently great.

IX.—Is it to be supposed that the people will prefer what they know is transient and cheap? Do you expect that they will defer to the learned after they themselves have read books; that they will take counsel of Crœsus after they know how millions are made and have traced the processes; or that they will adore successful warriors when fighting has become safe to those who know how to manage the machines, and they themselves know how? Is it not plain that men have always given their homage only to the persons and things that have stood for the immeasurable—the infinite; that scholars have been looked up to because books and brains were a mystery; rich men, because riches were supposed to go with godlike

The Religion of Democracy.

gifts and manners; and fighters, because they died fighting?

Sic transit gloria mundi! Now that it has been discovered with how little wisdom the world is governed, what fresh adventure is left to a man of spirit but to be honest and to believe in God!

X.—The old order is passing, and the new is swiftly preparing. It is nothing that the incapable and those that fail are discontented. If that were all, there might indeed be social changes—even what is called a revolution; but it would be only an oscillation, a vicissitude, a jar. There might be a new distribution of gains and honors; some would get more of praise and money than had been the former wont, and some less. But the old order, the world of the self-made man, would abide after all. The money and the honors would go to those that were strong and cunning enough to get and keep them, and the foundation of the social peace would rest upon things in sight, the phenomenal, the transient, as of old. It is nothing that those who fail are discontented; they always, alas! were discontented. But now those also that can move things and prevail are smitten at the heart, and restless; the successful are

The Religion of Democracy.

discontented with their success. That is of great omen. Not passionate, vacillating, incoherent *sans culotterie* alone is in revolt, but the principled, punctual world-power is insurgent against itself—a quite unprecedented state of things. There will be great changes—the making of a new world. The little revolutions are little because they begin at the bottom, and essay to run up; but the great revolution of the world begins at the top and, in the course of nature, runs, gathering mightily, down. But do not mistake the upper classes. They are the people that can steadily will. They do not necessarily live on the avenues, or have five courses at dinner. They are the youth of the world, and the people of sound nerves, those that have courage and that grip the real things. These are holding indignation meetings everywhere to protest against their own prosperity. It is an augury of the very greatest event—the revolution of revolutions.

For history can know but one great revolution. Only once can the world turn prodigiously on its moral axis, shifting its center of gravity from the temporal to the eternal. It has taken thousands of years to prepare for this, and it may take as many thousand more to fulfill it. But there is a moment in time,

The Religion of Democracy.

a supremely critical moment, when the scale turns.

A featherweight may turn the balance of tons, and a footfall on the mountain may start an avalanche. So the grand crisis of the world may come and go, and the occasion be not other than a little thing.

XI.—We see the old order—the *régime* of the self-made man—in the latter degrees of decrepitude. It is sick to exhaustion. Its pride is flouted in the streets and its props are decaying. The people do not have respect for dignities any more, and they cannot any longer be ruled by dignities.

Aristocracy has had its gifts and virtues. One is sorry to see them go—rather, one would be sorry if one really supposed that they were going; that other than the clothes and skins of them were going. And since the people do not now care for these brave, fair-showing things, and will not give them reverence, let us weep for the loss of beauty, having first made sure that beauty is really lost.

Democracy has shown ugly features; there have been times when one might have wished it out of the world. It has ruined many good pictures, broken acres of painted windows and corrupted court manners to a common level. A satyr-hoof has been in all the rose gardens, and has raped away the stately graces that strolled upon the terraces.

XII.—But there are grounds of thrilling hope. The destruction of the symbols of glory makes way for what is glorious. And what, after all, is glorious, but fearless, free spirits that dare everything for love!

Democracy has such in store. They will come to the relief of the saintless, poetless nations, before all the islands of the sea are tossed to the bargain counter, and the cities are wasted with war.

Out of democracy shall come poets, saints, artists, world-lovers of an unprecedented kind. How do we know? They will come because it is necessary.

XIII.—The world has had enough and has come to the end of that blighting, consumptive quality of democracy which has gone so far to make the world seem a moral wilderness, arid and flowerless of beauty. Democracy has razed temples and palaces; let us see now what it can build! We have had the Nay of it; we await the Yea. It has advertised the things

The Religion of Democracy.

that are *not* great; its pressing engagement now is to disclose the things that *are*. It has set its brand on pride and privilege, the boast and pomp of rank and honor—marked for destruction the glory of this world. It is time for the revelation of the greater glory.

We have had the law; we expect now the gospel of democracy. So far it has been Mosaic, prohibitive—its message mainly a "Thou shalt not." It has despised old shams, but it has not invented new valors. It has put down the mighty, but it has not made the commons royal. It has withheld its trust from princes; but it has not known where else to put its trust.

The people are sick of negations; it is necessary that the poets and the artists should come. The world has lost interest in the discouraging theorem that one man is no better than another. Nor does it find satisfaction in the rule of the majority. There is no advantage in being bullied by a crowd. The democracy of blank negations is played out.

XIV.—Yes, let us confess it plainly, if democracy contained what the politicians have said that it contains, and nothing more, it would be an entirely hopeless enterprise—the climax of unreason, the apotheosis of the absurd, the con-

The Religion of Democracy.

summate delusion of history, the destruction of every sweet and human thing, and the end of the world.

Were it not better to be a peasant and reverence a lord, than be a politician and reverence nothing?

Democracy, regarded as a balloting contrivance for equating the hoof and claw of warring private interests, is an ingenious futility. Let it pass now to its place in the museums of antiquities along with the devices for the solution of impossible mechanical problems, like that of perpetual motion.

The old aristocratic idea had more blood in it than that, and was more nearly a real and credible thing. A lord, a peasant, a priest—good enough, if only the lord had fed the peasant, and the priest had reverenced his soul; but since the peasant fed the lord and had to himself all the reverence in his own narrow, glimmering heart, he grew and lightened, and came to be at length himself both lord and priest! That is the authentic biology of democracy. Democracy is born out of the abyss of the infinite. It answers to the longing for beauty, the hunger and thirst after righteousness. If always men must live from hand to mouth, must dodge and calculate and gain by frugal shifts,

The Religion of Democracy.

then the self-made man must always win, and his sordid customs must be set up for good as the standard of the soul. But if it should turn out that a common man may have access to the springs of beauty and the eternal health, may look out upon the universal landscape from a commanding point of view and see things in their proportions, may cease to have mere static relations to the cosmos, and may establish dynamic and vital relations, why, then, it is all over with tyrannies and vested privileges. Status must give way to the dynamic laws; the arbitrary must yield to the essential. This is scientific; it is the ultimatum of the modern spirit. In the presence of the natural facts we are not interested in the things that were agreed upon. Etiquette, custom, the maxims of the wise and prudent, tradition, politics and the Revised Statutes —must make way for the elemental forces.

The social constitution becomes a *pis aller*. Let it wear for a week and then we shall get a better. We hold the civil laws lightly, because we perceive that they are only approximate; we shall get nearer the facts by and by. The beginning of democracy is the discovery that morality is not an appendix, but the bulk of the volume of natural philosophy—that righteous-

The Religion of Democracy.

ness is as large as all outdoors. The *Magna Charta* of democracy is the revelation of the immediate accessibility of God. It is a scandal to the ecclesiastics, politicians and bookmen because it makes faith the mother of science, and, in the scale of human faculties, gives the primacy not to the intellect, but to the will. It refuses to stop to think out a way to right living, but will go ahead to live out a way to right thinking. There is in it a stored, balked and latent energy to transform the world in a year. Democracy is born out of the brooding sense of the eternal; it takes up the message of the timeless Man of Nazareth; it will be true to the great evangel of Reformation and Renaissance from which Church and State have apostatized; it will put to confusion every ecclesiastic, dynastic and diplomatic scheme, and bring the nations together out-of-doors, in the eternal open air.

XV.—The new century opens with great expectancy. The future is full of charm. The past is past, and the children of the age are glad. There stretches before them an alluring, radiant vista, though the dawn dazzles their eyes, and they cannot clearly distinguish even what is near. No matter; they are not afraid.

The Religion of Democracy.

The stupefying spell of custom has been broken. The conspiracy of hebetude has been betrayed. Ideas, colossal, magnificent, are in the saddle, and are sailing the sea in ships. There is thunder in the air and ozone.

Oh! democracy of dead lift and suction, democracy of pull and haul, of covetousness, cautiousness and cunning, they give you up at last. You are not worth while. And your sapless platitudes, your sentimental pieties and patriotisms, they spew them out!

Allons! A new democracy—yet the oldest—shall renew the world; a democracy that shall not exclude foreigners or those that do not speak English; that shall take the earth to be its colony and the cosmic laws for statutes and ordinances. The Philippines, the Antilles and all the other islands of the sea, and the continents, coast-lands and hinter-lands, they shall all be taken in. We announce the dissolution of the old *régime* of privilege, exclusion and monopoly, and we proclaim a new constitution according to the essential law.

The Religion of Democracy.

CHAPTER IV.

THE DISCOVERY OF AMERICA.

I.—THIS land, America, shall be the land of the incarnation. On this ground the ideal is to come to terms with what is common and matter-of-fact. Here, on a grand scale, for the first time, labor shall be accepted without shame and death without fear. This shall be the country of material things, the land of the universal sacrament. We perceive that God does nothing for a show, or to prove propositions, or just to save souls; therefore we will have no art for the sake of art, we will not be governed by preaching, and we will do everything for utility, as God does. This shall be the land of commerce and manufacture; the land of money and credit, of the painters of pictures, the writers of books, and the carvers of statues for utility and the sweetening of the earth. We reject Utopias and abstract propositions. We will have no thinkers that do not dig, and no diggers that do not think.

The Religion of Democracy.

America shall be, we hope, the land of the open and flowing sea—the land of ships, of universal exchange; the builder of roads through the remote places, and of interoceanic canals; the destroyer of political boundaries.

This shall be the land of change, flux, progress; everything must flow. We will have nothing fixed and settled, since nothing in nature is fixed and settled—not the ribs of the earth nor the anatomy of a man. We take everything to be plastic, and we do not think that any beautiful thing is impossible. We expect the miraculous according to the ordinary run.

This shall be the land of modernity and the present day. We will not judge this day by the old times, but we will judge the old time from this eminence. We are interested to hear of anything that the fathers did freely and unprecedentedly; but what they did in the way of habit and reflex action we will note at first hand in the common animals.

We know that this day has lasted from the beginning, and will last; we are not disconcerted by sleep or the sunsets! We will regard everything from the eternal point of view.

II.—The grand event of the century dawn shall be the discovery of America. America

The Religion of Democracy.

—brooding in the old world spell, under fogbanks of tradition and habit—at last shall lift up its sunlit Sierras out of the mist and stand revealed to Europe and to itself.

It is said that America is to stand forth as an equal partner among what are called the Great Powers, that now at length she is to rise to the level of the jealousy and fear of Europe, and to clutch at her distributive share in the partition of Asia, Africa and the islands; that she is to produce statesmen and soldiers on the European model, and generally that she is to go ahead of what is going.

We do not think that America is to be revealed in that character. We do not believe that the mission of the United States is just to do better than its competitors the things that are being done. We look for new enterprise, and a *renaissance*, the discovery of a new world.

It is childish to suppose that we ever have been, or could be separated from Europe. The meaning of this epoch is not that the United States, long isolated, is now at length to make connection with the transatlantic world; nor is it that America, thralled in European bondage, is now at length to break away. The meaning of the epoch is the transfer of the moral

The Religion of Democracy.

hegemony of the world from the East to the West, from the romantic, earth-spurning, tipsy morning lands, the lands of prince and priest and soldier, of castle-building and Babel towers, to the lands of the sobering sunsets, of labor and science and strong, resurgent youth—in a word, from Aristocracy to Democracy.

It is not that Europe is to fade away and be but the evening shadows of the Western hills, nor that the East has definitely failed, nor that the West has now an advantage. It is not that Americans are generally good and wise, and Europeans bad and foolish. But this is the *dénouement* of a world-drama in which all are equally concerned. And there is in this tall, rude, prodigal West, a youth that has been in the wilderness, and has slept on the ground; that has been angered and has not been unforgiving; learned humor and humility and grown strong by labor; and he is now to play a great *rôle* of faith and redemption for the saving of the nations.

III.—We cannot be separated from the rest. In spite of tariffs, the illimitable seas and all the old ethnic jealousies and exclusions, the world has all things common. Whatever happens to one man, happens to everybody. You cannot

The Religion of Democracy.

take your tea and be careless of the coolies. You would have to settle with them anyhow in a thousand years. You must settle a great deal sooner now, considering the regularity of the mails and the facilities of circulation.

There is no social question anywhere that is not in the United States. There is no sort of tyranny, profligacy, or hardness of heart in any other country that is not here. The great contradiction of the age is wrought out here as it is in Europe. Here, as there, the old order, the *régime* of pride and privileges, is still lofty-looking, however desperately stricken with years and however fearsomely arrayed against the invincible standards of democracy.

IV.—There is no doubt that democracy—or something that goes by that name—will everywhere prevail. But it might be as the prevalence of hell were it not for the youth and faith in the heart of America.

The choice lies between the democracy of envy and *émeutes*, the lust for a dead level, always distractedly sought after, but never achievable in this world, and making all things beautiful forever unachievable, a desperate pendulum-swing between triumphant mercantilism and fierce, disruptive intestine wars; the choice

The Religion of Democracy.

lies between this and the parturition-pain of a new and unexampled world-order, a democracy of inner and sacramental equality, begotten of the modern sense of the eternal, and realizing itself in an elation of labor and commerce, in joyous, creative art, in wide-embracing comradeships, and a new taste in living. Expectation and the preparation for this event are everywhere latent, wistful, passive; but in the United States is the active principle of it, the genetic, begetting power. That principle and power is the unconscious embryonic soul of America, which now is brought forth in the shock of war, and which shall come to know itself and understand its destination. What but the greatest things can come of the nation that has conceived the idea of the sacredness of labor, and that has sincerely expected prophets from the back-country, and salvation out of Nazareth! This inspiration is not of the old order of things, nor by any means to be conciliated therewith. It is a blast of destruction for the old order, and a breath of creation for the new.

V.—The motive of the old *régime*, the spring of its energy, the explanation of what we have chosen to call its virtues and what we have chosen to call its vices, is, as has been said, the

The Religion of Democracy.

endeavor to escape into an ideal world. The masters of the old *régime*, the admired and influential men, are the agents and examplars of glory, terrestrial or celestial—in a word, the soldiers and the priests.

The energy of the new *régime* arises in an opposite quarter and runs the other way, so that the two systems are at utter variance and can never come to terms.

The power of the new order, the *élan* of the modern spirit, comes of taking the ideal world for granted and proceeding, in the faith of it, to the conquest of the real. The soldier and the priest fall back, and the artist, the mechanic, and the man of business become the masters of society.

The historic symbol and prophecy of this great transaction—by no means yet fully accomplished, but awaiting fulfillment in the newly-discovered West—is that epochal moment when the Middle Ages began to be modern with the decline of the feudal powers and the rise of the free cities of art and commerce. The burghers came to be more considerable than knights and friars, not because the Crusades had utterly failed, but because they had not utterly failed; not because men had abandoned the desire for the beautiful and settled

The Religion of Democracy.

down to be sordid, but because they had found and fastened upon somewhat of the beautiful, and were determined to put it to use—determined to make the cities *free*. It was a great moment, the beginning of the visible prevalence of the modern spirit. The gains may seem to have been small and easily lost; but they were not lost. The world sometimes moves slowly, and the road seems long, but the burghers had set out hopefully on the way that leads from Nazareth to the cosmopolitan city of the soul.

Ever since the rise of the Italian and Hanseatic commercial towns the man of business has gained upon the politician and the ecclesiastic, upon the soldier and the priest. Spite of all his undeserving, spite of usury, luxury, extortion and monopoly, spite of the valor of soldiers and the love of saints, he has gained. He has gained because he is in the way of the destiny of the world. Up to this time the man of business has, to speak broadly, done his best to miss his opportunity; but the opportunity remains. Nay! the end of the century presents to him an occasion that not only invites, but also commands and threatens. Now at last the business man must, on dreadful pains and penalties, get down to business—must stop his ears to the brandishments of old world oracles, and com-

The Religion of Democracy.

mit himself fearlessly to the new world mission. The trouble has been that the man of business has not believed in his calling; he has deferred to priests and soldiers; he has caught the contagion of the dreams of glory-seekers. His mind has been elsewhere than on his work. He has fed the hungry, some of them, and clothed the naked abstractedly; he has tamed fierce wildernesses, but he has not cared for the people that should inhabit them; he has built ships, railroads, Suez canals, in an absent-minded way, thinking of other things, of money, power, politics, social esteem, caste, colleges, carriages. We have not yet seen a modern man of business. We have had merchant princes to spare, but not yet a prince of merchants. Perhaps, after all, the priests and soldiers had better turn traders and engineers, and let the mooning men of business, for a while, tell the beads and wear the gilded sashes.

VI.—It has been supposed that we could first settle the bread question, and then proceed to finer issues. But there are no finer issues—there is nothing finer than common bread, unless it be bread of a finer kind; or than a cup of water, unless it be a cup of wine. The palpable, real world is unfathomable, mysterious,

The Religion of Democracy.

spiritual, and there is room in it for the most magnificent adventure of the ideal. It is not necessary to go apart from it in order to think or to aspire; the dignity of thinking is in labor, and the dignity of labor in thinking. The sphere of economics is without bounds; it takes in all the fine arts and the unnamed finer arts, and there is no magnanimity or love that cannot be expressed somehow in terms of bread and wine.

It is common to speak of the laws of nature, of chemistry, biology, and so on, as if they were distinguishable from the essential moral laws. But they are not local shifts; they are not other than the essential, moral laws, and there is no natural law or section, or sub-title of a law that does not exist for the sake of the liberty of the soul. The question of food and clothes is inextricably bound up with the interests of art and letters, and all together are meshed and woven in with the grand, eternal issues, so that we cannot make an inch of progress in the settlement of economic questions save as we make progress in the settlement of the other questions.

We have had a theory in America that we could first lay a solid foundation of economic prosperity, that we could proceed then to litera-

The Religion of Democracy.

ture and art galleries, and finish up with cathedrals and religion. The religious specialists will tell us that all this is exactly preposterous; that the progression must begin at the other end, and run in the other direction. But these nice discussions are out of date. The day dawns for the lovers, and the men of action, who have souls to their bodies, and bodies to their souls, and are not too curious about the distinction.

VII.—Not without travail the new nation is born. In vast transportations over seas, in hot, malarial campaigns, in Malaysian and West Indian jungles, in battles not all a holiday and gay in victories, America breaks through its integumentary barriers of protective tariffs, immigration acts, *passé* presidential doctrines, hypocritical neutralities, and wins out into the wind-swept highways of the world. Through the swinging Janus gates the youth and faith of America go forth as not knowing whither, yet going East and West, following the equator and the tropics, until they shall somehow meet and girdle the earth and embrace it. Once more, after four hundred years, the galleons of Spain have sailed West, and discovered a world!

The Religion of Democracy.

VIII.—Universality, unanimity! America shall be the crossroads of the world. The nations shall flow into it, and pass through it. We renounce old habits. We have no patent on democracy; we will not make the abolition of privilege itself a privilege.

We will make here a clearance of every law-made privilege and monopoly, and we will make it intolerably hard for other countries to maintain privileges and monopolies. There shall be newspapers at length and universities, and there shall be ideas that march. We know that we cannot win liberty or justice for one country without winning it for all countries; that to lift one is to lift all, that the load is an Atlas-load. But the shoulders of democracy are broad.

Bonaparte announced at the beginning of the century *la carrière verte aux talents*. What he meant was a free course for men of brains. The men of brains have had their day, and we see what they have done for us. America offers at the end of the century a career for men of faith.

The invitation is not for those that would like in the intervals of other business to do what is called a little good, but for those that love the risks of faith and the divine adventure, that

The Religion of Democracy.

know the release and expansion of a lover, and can lose themselves in their enterprise, and live hard and like it. For such there is a clear vocation and a career. It is no smooth boulevard, no lounger's promenade: it is a rugged, narrow path through the world chaos; but it is a highway of great discovery.

CHAPTER V.

THE DISCOUNT OF GLORY.

I.—IN the harbor of Manila, at Santiago de Cuba, and elsewhere, the guns of the old *régime* slacken their fire and are silenced. In the way of powder, steel and fighting machines, the old order has not now any great hope. War becomes a kind of inverted manufacture, a grim, terrific commerce. The Soldier and the Priest have no longer a chance in this pursuit against the Mechanic and the Man-of-business. It is demonstrated that a democracy a little faithful to its charter of humility would be invincible against the pompous armaments of the world. The meekness of mechanics shall make the Powers powerless. Bulk is nothing; but to know how things go in this God's world is something. To be *en rapport* with the universe, to have the *feel* of it in your bones and the law of it leaping in your blood—that is everything in modern war.

Ten thousand men with cosmic justice in

The Religion of Democracy.

them, the divine *entente* with Nature's soul, could put the whole big, blustering world to ignominious rout.

They could do it; but they would not. For this cosmic justice, this miracle behind mechanics, is magnanimity and love. The meekness that is might is also mercy. And when winning comes to be too easy and too safe, it will cease to seem so glorious. A few more victories like that of Dewey and Sampson, and Victory herself will be smitten with a kind of shame, and will appoint days of fasting in love and pity for her enemies.

II.—America is strong and can win battles because of its labor and its earth-grip; because of its mechanics that can build a ship or punctually sink one with simple and loving devotion, but it is not invincible; it is weak because of its sentimental abstractions, its longing for privileges and glory, its passion for prize money. The enemy was weak in ships; but his death-clutch held us close, and he is strong in virulent contagion. Rome revenged herself on her conquerors by corrupting them, and so Spain, too, may get revenge—may infect us with the full fire and venom of the old-world glory disease.

The Religion of Democracy.

It was a dramatic thing—so subtle and sure is the inner logic of history—this wrestle on the threshold of the new era, of the young giant of democracy with the choicest champion and Paladin of the ancient *régime*. Spain, the classic land of the soldier and the priest, ultra-undemocratic Spain, the country that least believes in the intrinsic justice and reasonableness of the real world, and most believes in things-agreed-upon, in honor, orthodoxy, and authority—Spain, the arch-agent and exemplar of the great political and ecclesiastical superstition, was well matched in mortal combat with the democratic land.

It is a conflict the issues of which are to be lifted up and graven high; but the firing of guns was incidental. The allies of Spain are not mostly Spaniards. Everywhere through the Rockies and the Alleghenies, by the Mississippi, the Hudson and the Potomac, the soil of democracy teems with a kind of treason, albeit a kind that is not a crime in law. It fills the newspapers and magazines, and Ferdinand and St. Ignatius Loyola from congenial constituencies have got themselves sent to congress. No man can say to another: you are a spy, because in every man, the accuser as well as the accused, there is a conspirator against the sover-

The Religion of Democracy.

eignty of the outdoors God, a prebendary of the old *régime* pleading for honors and privileges, for Pope-holy pieties and patriotisms, against the liberal, open-air view of things, which is democracy.

III.—The thing that has been most steadily desired since the world began is not money, or long life, or pleasant pastimes, but a guaranteed god—a god with solid, institutional backing, advertising himself in distinct terms, and plainly discriminating between deserving persons and nations, and the undeserving.

Disappointments have been heaped up from age to age; but every turn of the world has found the people newly disposed to believe that God has established himself at last and settled down in some high political, scholastic, or ecclesiastical seat, so that the divine judgment on human conduct can be obviously and immediately translated into brands of infamy and medals of honor.

It is this longing for an unquestionably respectable and plain-spoken God that has been the stronghold of all the monarchies, aristocracies and ecclesiocracies of the world. The privileged classes have kept their privileges and have ruled the people not only or chiefly on account of their superior wisdom and strength, but because they have been supposed to be the special backers and spokesmen of God. Their ribbons, and title-givings, their blessings and anointings have seemed to be veritable means of grace and bestowments of spiritual power, because it has been supposed that the givers were the depositaries of peculiar and incommunicable divine revelations; that they stood nearer God than the people did, and nearer than the people could. Back of every social organization under the old *régime* is some kind of supposed guaranteed revelation of God, some form of denial of the fundamental democratic doctrine of the utter commonness of revelation. The modern spirit is in these days lifting up its voice to bear witness against every pretension of those that claim a right to speak conclusively for God. Democracy cannot come to any kind of terms with specially guaranteed revelations. For such things, whether interpreted by priests and princes, or by scribes and doctors, mean the establishment of authority outside the conscience of the people—mean, in a word, the negation of self-government.

IV.—Infinitely pathetic and man-endearing is the heartbreak of the hundred ages, this

The Religion of Democracy.

alienation of the old world from the God of the open air. One would think that sometimes, in moments like this, when the strain is great, God would long to break the interminable silence and tell us plainly, in some prodigious and undeniable way, that this is the soul's world, and that we need not be afraid. Doubtless he does so long, and his withholding is a continual passion.

Certainly the righteousness, the moral sympathy, of the universe does not impose itself upon us—it is not undeniable. We are left free to believe that the whole scheme is bad or unfeeling, and that the God of it is not our God. There is a silence in it that seems like indifference, and a hardness that seems like wickedness, and contradictions that look unreasonable. For thousands of years we have stood off at a distance, lynx-eyed, inquisitive, suspicious, and tried to construe it to the understanding to see it steady and whole in logical perspective; but nobody has yet succeeded in doing that. There is always an unassimilable remainder, a surd. It is not always possible to turn away and say: "I do not find myself here. I will get my living out of this, since I must; but I will live in another, an ideal world." So thick are the veils, so patiently does God hide his

The Religion of Democracy.

face, that men may believe without compulsion, may achieve original love and be free.

It is a part of the ground plan of the world that it should be always possible to doubt the safety of doing what is beautiful and right, possible to doubt whether the ultimate authorities of the universe would back one up in that kind of enterprise. It seems that tonic, drastic doubt is forever necessary in order that beauty and right should grow indigenous in man. The measure of the beautifulness in a man is the amount of ugliness that he can meet without despairing, and the dignity of the stature of his faith is in proportion to the clearness and sanity with which he doubts. The man of the modern spirit is a mighty doubter; and the depth of his Gethsemane measures the height of his Golgotha.

The death of religion is in a dead certainty. Perhaps God would sooner destroy all the Bibles of the nations and efface all the miracles of faith, than remove the possibility of that spirit-stirring doubt.

V.—It is not that God has filled the earth with little traps to catch us and perplex us. The question of faith is not a matter of the preponderance of evidence—beak and claws on one

The Religion of Democracy.

side, rosebuds and summer on the other. It is perceived that since all things hang together, one thing must be as good as another, and no better. The doubt spreads over all and takes in everything.

Looked at in the way of this all-comprehending doubt, the world seems to the moral sense a desert swept clean by the wind of every footprint of divinity; there are no exceptional phenomena, no oases; all is sapless, siccate, bare. There is no meaning in the patient valor of Jesus, the suffering of the poor, the ineffable charm of womanliness and manliness, the great poems and pictures, the grand rituals of worship; there is left only the opportunity to improve one's own mind and better one's condition. Yea, the last marvel of nature and its furthest reach toward the infinite is just a curious, selective mind whereby you may accellerate the process of your making. You are the choicest, quintessent creature!

From all this the soul of a man turns away in bitterness. If he is nothing but the Finest Thing Made, then it is all over with religion and great art, and it is all over with magnanimity and valor.

VI.—You may choose to look at things so if

The Religion of Democracy.

you will; or if you will the world may roll out its landscape in another light. You find in yourself a witness that you are not altogether made but are also maker. This seems a voucher of eternity. You see yourself not as the last term in a process of development, but the first term. You date back of Abraham, back also of the amœba. You rise up from your passivity; you cease to wish and begin to will. You claim a share in the business and passion of creation. This is faith; it is also the principal of democracy. It is the assertion, in spite of doubt, that the sovereignty of God is in some real sense within yourself, and so in conflict with the disorder and brutality of the world you are like a king contending for your own kingdom. You back up against the impregnable eternities, and are ready to die a thousand deaths for what to the soul seems sweet and just.

VII.—Always this antithesis of doubt and faith has, in terms more or less distinct, been presented to the souls of men; and the antithesis will doubtless stand.

After thousands of years of investigating and philosophizing the *savants* have at last in these latter days got the case approximately stated

The Religion of Democracy.

—which is a gain, perhaps the greatest gain of the century. But the men of action and the mass of the people were a long way in advance of them in the discovery of the fact—the fact that the antithesis exists, and that it is unescapable and irreducible.

The discovery of this inexpugnable doubt is the negative power of the modern spirit. Herein at last is one thing logically settled—to wit, that the final issue of life is not capable of logical settlement must be allowed to remain, so far as mere intellect goes, an open question. There is no blackboard demonstration that God is good; you must risk it, or die a coward. There is no earthly help for you; you cannot shift the responsibility. There is no insurance society that can guarantee you against loss; there is no prize-money promise of the ruling powers that the general government of the world may not at last, after all, repudiate.

No extant person, natural, legal or mystical, is qualified to assume your soul. God has decided to withhold himself, and has appointed no agents with power of attorney. The corporations that pretend to the function of blessing and cursing, rewarding and punishing, are not authentic. The authority of the Church becomes a fading specter and the sovereignty of

The Religion of Democracy.

the State a legal fiction. There is only one sovereignty, and its exterritoriality is, for this day, in your own body. You are to make your report, not to the majority, or to the ordained and the anointed, but to that.

God withholds himself, and there is on this earth no sure fountain of salvation or honor. The Church can excommunicate, but it cannot effectually exclude; the State can crucify, but it cannot convict. There are instituted powers, but there are no instituted authorities. One may be hanged, drawn and quartered, perhaps with good desert; but he cannot, here, be judged.

The Judge and Rewarder has not in Church or State, or anywhere save in conscience and the common, cosmic law, set up here His court.

VIII.—These things follow from the discovery of the invincible doubt; the discovery that the final issue is deep down in the core of consciousness, where the everlasting yea and nay are met, that the final question cannot be resolved by the understanding, but must be encountered, and somehow practically determined by the will. This discovery is a cardinal revelation, because it clears the road for faith. Faith could never have been in this world if the scribes and doctors had had their cock-sure way. It would have been impossible for the people to trust in God if the authorities had not been first discredited. If it had been perfectly certain that the overwhelming presence of God was at Mt. Sinai, there would have been place for fidelity and endless deference, but not of faith. Moses himself was not quite sure, else he would not so command our reverence. And all along the old heathen and Hebrew ways in the dust of the unremembered throng that were convinced of Moses' law or Moloch's, are the vestiges of loving and valiant souls that were not quite sure of the oracle, and were fain to trust in God.

IX.—It is the distinction of the Jews, that they were from of old comparatively modern. Might not one say that modernity itself is of the Jews? They were the best doubters in antiquity, and accordingly had most of faith. Less than their neighbors did they concern themselves with what is called the future life, and they looked not for rewards and penalties from thence. The insoluble questions they were content to leave insoluble. They did not expect salvation or honor from an institution. Their immortal glory is that they did not thirst for glory; and they were the only first-class power of the ancient world that did not found an empire. They were of all the least sentimental, and had the least of superstition. Even to this day, when modernity itself seems wavering, and in religion and politics, in art and letters, is meditating a retreat to Mediævalism, or further back, the Jews go bravely on their mission, freest of the taint of morbid ideality and most exposed to the fury of enthusiastic wrong.

The genius of the Jews is of the concrete only. There is in it a sterling realism, a manly, quick settlement of accounts. Their world-mission has been to witness for the intrinsicality, the self-sufficiency of right, against every sort of spiritual dodge and shift, and *deus ex machina*.

The Jewish Scriptures are shot through from beginning to end with this idea. It is the principle that grips the Old Testament with the New, and co-ordinates their seeming contradictions. Right, in the Bible, is never a bitter thing, which, if you will take you shall have sweet things for bonus. The right of the Jewish Scriptures is always sweet and desirable, and proves itself as it goes. In the Old Testament are manna, milk and honey, purple and fine linen, flocks and herds and length of days in the New Testament there are other and different things that it takes more of a man to come up with; but there is never anywhere a suspended payment or a getting ahead of God, no works of supererogation, no meritorious services, no honors or titles, no ribbons or medals, no extraneous glory, no prize money. One plants and digs and gets corn and wine, but not testimonials or promotions. The blessings and cursings do not count against the law; everything goes to its own place.

The faith of the Bible is not a conviction about God, a conclusion stubbornly stuck to, or dictated by authority. It is not a conviction at all; it is a willingness, a resolution to take risk that this world really is at bottom what it ought to be, and that it can in its very nature fulfill the heart's longing. Jesus spoke with authority to the Jews, precisely because he spoke from this ground of the intrinsic and elemental, and did not speak as the authorities did. It would have been different in the Forum or Areopagus among the worshipers of an emperor or the partisans of philosophers. There were more Pharisees in Rome or in Athens than there were in Jerusalem, more men with an obsession, more victims of an ideal.

The Religion of Democracy.

The excellence of the Jews was their superior sanity and earth-fitness. It was by no accident that the typical modern man was born a Jew, and that he spoke not to the people whose inspirations were the exquisite, wistful imagining of Homer or Virgil, but to those whose poems were full of labor and migrations and patient waiting, of the laying out of the land, the rearing of children, and the acquisition of flocks and herds. The great men of Jewish literature were neither priests nor soldiers, but economists and men of affairs—Abraham, Isaac and Jacob. And these were admired not for their performances—their fame abashed nobody—but for their method, their faith which was understood to be equally available for all. Thus caste was excluded with the sentimentalities of hero worship and the blind devotions of royalty. Men were put in possession of themselves, and the way was cleared for the evangel of modern democracy.

The Jewish people were the religious people *par excellence*, simply because they did not make religion a specialty, and did not occupy themselves with vain questions concerning the immortality of the soul. The progress of religion throughout the ages has consisted in withdrawing men's minds from another world to

The Religion of Democracy.

this; it is the passing of the hope of immortality into the present sense of eternity.

Materialism is the raw material of religion. In all times the enemy of faith has been, not carnality and worldliness, but a strained and distempered ideality—a longing for a mystical or artificial world-order whose law should be other than the law of the present world—a pruriency of ecclesiastic or imperialistic ambition. The defenders of the faith have made it hard to believe in God; and the champions of an imperial order have cast us into a wilderness of politics. The cruelest men have been the makers of empires, as Napoleon and Philip II. of Spain — excepting only the makers of churches, as Torquemada and Calvin. God will have sons. And the twentieth century belongs neither to the priests nor to the politicians.

X.—The mission of democracy is to put down the rule of the mob. In monarchies and aristocracies it is the mob that rules. It is puerile to suppose that kingdoms are made by kings. The king would do nothing if the mob did not throw up its cap when the king rides by. The king is consented to by the mob because of that in him which is mob-like. The

The Religion of Democracy.

mob loves glory and prizes; so does the king. If he loved beauty and justice, the mob would shout for him while the fine words were sounding in the air; but he could never celebrate a jubilee or establish a dynasty. When the crowd gets ready to demand justice and beauty, it becomes a democracy and has done with kings.

The crowd is protoplasmic; it is the raw material of humanity. It is in process of being made; it has not yet acquired status as maker. It is passive and yields to every suggestion. It wishes, but hardly wills. For the most part, indeed, it follows the suggestions of nature and the immanent God. It performs marvelous feats of wisdom and devotion, because of its utter receptivity. It makes languages, invents words whose insight surpasses all philosophy, suffers prodigies of toil and fights great battles. But it is capable also of every infamy and atrocity if conjured thereto in the name of patriotism, liberty, or any other well-sounding word.

The crowd, touched with morbid ideality, becomes the mob. A mob is the crowd corrupted by unrealizable abstractions. The September massacres in Paris and St. Bartholomew's day are corollaries of the divine right of kings and priests. A slum is the reflection—in a puddle —of the dilettanteism of drawing rooms and the cant of sectarian churches; as a museum of horrors is of like inspiration with a charity ball. Both make a pomp of misery and shame.

XI.—Psychologically speaking, it is the definition of the old *régime* that therein the practical understanding which proceeds from the will is subordinated to the faculty of passive thinking—call it intuition, cognition, reflection, abstraction, pure reason, as you like—which proceeds from the emotions, from that in a man wherein he is moved, but is not a mover. The strife of the ages is to get this order reversed, to master the thinking that reflects by the thinking that grapples with things and creates—the thinking that conceives ideals, by the thinking that achieves them.

The loftiest thing in a man is not his pure reason; it is in this that he draws nearest to the primal, passive, dream state of the undifferentiated crowd, and to the mind and instinct of animals. A man is a man not because his mind reflects the world with ideal variations; the mind of a dog does that. He growls in his dreams to prove himself capable of abstract and conceptual thinking. And every donkey is a master of inductive science and argues of carrots in general from particular carrots. A man is a man not because of his percepts or his concepts, but because he understands the world somewhat, believes in it, and will improve it.

To this general issue runs the monumental demonstration of Immanuel Kant, that unwitting expounder of revolutionary, democratic dialectic, the Copernicus of social philosophy, who, walking his prim, punctual way in his Königsberg garden has set the world a-spinning and turned things upside down. Civilization waits for the practical understanding to answer back and corroborate the reason and to fulfill the heart's desire. It is the response of the Son of God to the summons of the Father. From this proceed all proper human enterprise and wisdom. It is the essential human mind. The way of intellect is in labor and self-denial, the striving energy of creation. The typical act of intellect is an act of justice or the fashioning of a thing that is beautiful; and its axiom is the plasticity of all materials to what is best.

XII.—But the old *régime*—the *régime* of reflection, tradition, culture—is at the mercy of

The Religion of Democracy.

the mob because its axiom is that things are inevitably what they are; and it has nothing to offer to the god-thirst of the people but a swoon or a glory charm. The sway of "pure reason" is free swing for fanaticism and every fine frenzy. It is also the condition of solid, established tyranny, and the supremacy of dogma. It makes smooth the way for the strut of the pedant, the superciliousness of science for its own sake, and art for the sake of art. It is the rule of princes, priests, aristocrats, and sentimentalists. It is the rule of the mob, because the mob is in its rulers. The man that feels himself endowed with exclusive and peculiar rights to be royal, noble, religious, artistic or scientific is a visionary; the rapture and fanaticism of the mass is in him. He is not yet integrated and individualized; he has yet to become a self-governing person, a poet, an artist, a man of the people.

XIII.—The man of the modern spirit refuses to rule the people; he would rather die than do it. He gives his life that the people may rule themselves. He will not raise a flag, pronounce a shibboleth, or preach a crusade. He will not drive the people mad with a fine sentiment, or kill his enemies with an abstraction. He does not care for clans or gangs, for the union of

The Religion of Democracy.

labor, the communism of capital, or for any other kind of mobbery. We will make the masses men. He has set his heart not upon solidarity—the union of men in interest and sentiment—but upon unanimity, the union in faith and will; and he will dissolve every bulk and corporation that withstands him until he shall arrive there.

The Religion of Democracy.

CHAPTER V.

THE SOVEREIGNTY OF THE PEOPLE.

I.—To say that the sovereignty is in the people is the same as to say that the Kingdom of God is within you—which is the creed of the religion of democracy. It requires that every man shall be his own taskmaster, and it is the negation of every external and conventional authority. The life of government is force, and when a democratic man uses force he takes a personal responsibility, and will not shelter himself behind a governmental corporation. In that there is no sovereignty; the sovereignty is in the *man*. The justification of force is its justice; there is no longer any other available sanction. It is no longer necessary to be patriotic, or what is called in the cant of courtiers, loyal, but it is necessary to do what to you seems human, and to meet God. There is no power in the state to shrive you; how then dare you do the bidding of the state?

The Religion of Democracy.

This fiction of governmental sovereignty—snag of the old *régime*—sticks fast here in the soil of democracy; but it must, at whatever cost of sweat and blood, be rooted out. Vicksburg and Gettysburg have given their witness for the sovereignty of the people; and so, we trust, have Manila and Santiago de Cuba.

We have no right in the Spanish islands but human rights, and the sovereignty of the Spanish state has withstood us. But what have the people cared for that? Over the ruins of the Spanish state sovereignty the guns of the American people have saluted the enfranchised citizens of Spain. The people must do what is necessary to make this message good, though every gibbering ghost of European political witchcraft should rise up and menace in the way. For we have a greeting also for the people of Russia and France, the people of England, Italy, Germany and Austria; we have guns for a royal salutation to all the awakening peoples of the world. But Americans who talk of empire know not what manner of spirit they are of.

II.—They dream also who suppose that the Civil War was fought over a question of geography, like the old dynastic feuds. America

The Religion of Democracy.

did not spend a million lives of men for the sake of transferring the sovereignty of state from Richmond to Washington. The Civil War was the revolt of the people against the priests of politics; it defied the constitution and flouted every rite of legalism to free slaves. The Civil War was a revolution. It was followed, like every other revolution wrought in violence, by a recoil, a counter-revolution; and the old political superstition has thriven like a ghoul on the graves of the revolters.

Treason?—that is a word to be written by the side of heresy in the catalogue of crime. Both are relics of the old *régime.* A man may still be a rascal and a liar, but *leze majesty?*—it is unintelligible. If you run counter to the crowd you may be done to death, as in the old times, but we will not damn you by law. We do not pass bills of attainder any more, or bestow blessings and curses in statutes. There can be in a democracy no such thing as the crime of treason, unless indeed it be such to attempt to set up, over against the sovereignty of the people, a governmental corporation to keep their consciences. On the day that it ceased to be right to do a thing on the sole ground that the priest or the prince commanded it, the crime of treason and the crime of heresy became alike ab-

The Religion of Democracy.

surd. If John must judge for himself on peril of his soul, it is hardly reasonable to excommunicate him for judging against the crowd.

The Revised Statutes of the United States make it treason for an American to say anything to any foreign man and stranger that might make it harder for the American government to do whatever it may have in its mind to do. But the Revised Statutes are to be again revised.

Democracy lifts up its standard against both Guelph and Ghibelline, and sees not much difference between the politics of Ultramontanes and the Ultramontanism of politics.

III.—The radical idea of the sovereignty of government is unquestionable right and uncontrollable power lodged in some person or corporation whereunto the people must and ought to yield obedience. It is the product of a refined ecclesiastical philosophy, and by subtle implications it links to the temporal a kind of spiritual authority. It grew up out of the mediæval strife between Pope and Emperor, and reached its full bloom and perfection after Protestantism had bereft the people of their former spiritual masters. It is not necessarily associated with the divine right of kings; the di-

The Religion of Democracy.

vine right of parliaments, and popular majorities have served as well—just as Protestant church councils have served as well as the Pope to settle orthodoxy and punish heretics.

Of course the freshness has gone now from the bloom of the thing; and the sovereignty of the State to-day is only a faded remnant of what it has been in the past. It has become difficult to explain; the doctors of law write voluminous chapters about it, without making the matter clear. However, a historical principle may live on for a while, though the brains be out of it.

The practical effect of the tradition is the current theory of national solidarity which makes it disgraceful, if not a crime, for a citizen to dissent from the majority in any matter concerning the people that live outside the charmed circle of the national lot. Time was when such a notion was an ingenuous superstition; but it is difficult now to let it pass under that description. As a policy it is reactionary and anachronistic, and as a sentiment it seems to be cant.

This *en-bloc* theory of nationality makes the government responsible for the opinion and deportment of every citizen, on the good old-time principle—explicitly invoked by Washington and the fathers, with quotations from Vattel

The Religion of Democracy.

and the pundits—that the government is sovereign and the people subject, which is contrary to the fact as we understand it at the present day. Hence have come all the complexities of our neutrality laws, whereby the courts have arrived at length at the conclusion, worthy of the casuistry of mediæval schoolmen, that, whereas, an American patriot may with a clear conscience arm and equip a ship in an American port and sail away and sell it to a belligerent—providing always he do it strictly in the way of trade, and to turn a penny—it is, on the other hand, a felony to furnish a hod of coal if you do it for love of a cause.

IV.—The logic of national solidarity is a Chinese wall with stupidity and stoppage of the mail. Certainly without such helps it becomes impossible to keep peace between the nations. National solidarities, when they are permitted to meet, are mutually repellent and antagonistic. Loyalty becomes a synonym for moral lawlessness, the welter and confusion of irrational war. *Beati possidentes* is the law of nations, and diplomacy is a ruthless game. There is room in this world for not more than one sovereign and interiorly stolid state; but as suspicion breeds suspicion, so this sovereign-

The Religion of Democracy.

ty and solidarity begets a monster to destroy it. In America the natural gravitation of State sovereignty is to United States sovereignty; thence the road would lie to Anglo-Saxondom or Pan-Americandom, and so forth, until half the world should fall heavily upon the other half, and everything that is precious should be broken to pieces. After that we might begin the round again, and so on—world without end. But since this sovereignty of State cannnot love its enemies it never can save the world.

Democracy pays only a passing and provisional respect to the metes and bounds of nationalities. Blood is truly thicker than water; the nations are all of one blood, and rivers and oceans cannot divide them.

The people will have governments, as many as may be convenient and for as long a time as they are useful to defend the lives of the weak and the property of the poor, to arrest the robbers, run the mails, and make the cities glorious; but the people will not have sovereign governments for long. There was perhaps a time when devotion to the tribe was the way of the soul, leading to virtue and the humanities. Perhaps there was a time when the worship of a piece of land to the disparagement of the rest

The Religion of Democracy.

of the earth was economizable to moral ends. But that is past; it is not good—it is not in honesty possible to follow a tribe after one has met and known the brave men and sweet women of other tribes. And now there can be no holy or unholy ground, since after all we have left the sepulcher of the man of the modern world in the hands of the unbelievers.

The augurs of the political superstition may take their *rôle, au serieux;* but the people nudge one another as they pass them in the streets. A few more battles fought from habit and momentum, and European armies that confront each other with so grim and threatening an aspect will laugh out loud at the credulity of their masters, and fling themselves into each other's arms.

V.—The democracy of the new day does not despise government as such, or hold it under suspicion. It is not to be defined by any of the traditional theories of political liberty. It does not accept the doctrinaireism of Thomas Jefferson, nor does it philosophize with Stuart Mill. The liberty for which it strives is not a negation, the mere absence of restraint; it is the expansion and elevation of life in the realization of beauty and justice. And it would cook the people's food and wash their clothes by law, if liberty and justice should require it. It feels no shrinking from the use of force; its God is the God of energy and insistence, and His compulsions are in their way as good as His gifts and graces.

Democratic government is the concurrence of the most forceful and effective persons in society to the ends of beauty and justice. So long as the most forceful persons do not care for these things but prefer glory and privilege, democratic government is impossible, and we are left to the rule of an aristocracy of politicians and promoters, the dreariest aristocracy, on the whole, that the world has ever seen. Yet unquestionably these are, as yet, the most forceful persons, else they would not have their way.

Not what he can get by it, but what he would cheerfully lose for it, is the measure of a man's love of justice, and myriads of justice-seekers for the sake of the profits could never found or enforce a democratic government. They are wax in the hands of the politicians and promoters, because their spokesmen can be bought. Money rules because men are for sale. The gist of democratic government is the self-governing of the governors, and the warrant of

The Religion of Democracy.

their office is voluntary servitude. They must share the privation and exposure of the workers, and the spring of their power shall be that they breed in the people a love of justice. The people will love justice when they see justice—when they behold the beauty of it in the faces of men who prefer it to a privilege. The sovereignty of the people can be borne only by men who are of the people—men who will not have anything that all others may not have on the same terms.

VI.—Strictly speaking, democracy is the despair of politics and the destruction of politicians. The body of politics is privilege. Since civil government began one class has always preyed upon another, and that through the exercise of privilege legally guaranteed. The problem of the politicians has always been very simple in principle, although exceedingly complex in its practical presentment because of the infinite variation of circumstances. The problem is: How to make the social privileges coincide with the natural powers; or, in other words: How to so arrange matters that the social advantages shall tranquilly rest with those who have the natural power to maintain them.

If the sense of justice could be wholly elimi-

The Religion of Democracy.

nated from the human soul the problem of practical politics would be vastly simplified—the most stable state being that which is most sordid. But the sense of justice never has been eliminated, not even from the souls of politicians, and so the political problem, though commonly admitting of some kind of temporary adjustment, has become increasingly difficult, with the rise and prevalence of the modern spirit.

Among what are called the progressive peoples, the natural powers have never even for a moment been made to exactly coincide with the social privileges, because with the people the natural powers are in perpetual flux and change. Nature, in its long, slow processes, is on the side of justice, and so is forever bringing both privileges and politics to confusion. The most successful politicians are those most sensible of this flow of things; and they have devised systems adaptive and flexible, proclaiming in one form or another a career for talent, by which is meant a progressive apportionment of privileges according to the mutations of power. But the intrinsic justice of things has outwitted even these, through the operation of the principle, little regarded by politicians, that privilege is in its very nature

The Religion of Democracy.

weakening, that it tends to giddiness and abstraction, taking the *verve* and veracity out of men and rendering them incapable of dealing effectively with the world as it really is.

However, by one turn and another, by shift and compromise, and high exercise in a delicate art of balancing, the politicians have kept the saddle and have arrived upon the present scene. The point is that the continuation of their career depends upon the perpetuation of privilege. The destroyers of privilege shall unhorse the politicians and put an end to politics, clearing the way for a business-like administration by an improved kind of business men.

But privilege is the passion of the mob. The strength of it is not only in the oppressors, but also in the madness and folly of the oppressed. The soul of it is sentimentality, the impostures of Chauvinism, sectionalism and party loyalty, the repulsion for labor, and the desire to escape from the reality of the world. The destroyers of privilege must then be of stout fiber to hold the people to veracity, tough campaigners for whom a knapsack and a canteen will easily suffice. The administrators of democratic government must be canny men, craftsmen, artists and men of affairs, that can fix their minds upon the concrete, cut through the wilderness

The Religion of Democracy.

of fine sentiments, and bureaucratic formulas, and get things done.

VII.—Democratic government is the standing together of a multitude of men who could each stand alone. Its business is to balk the mob of the fraudulent gains of a sordid good-fellowship and to brace them to moral independence. As the scheme of the creation is the integrating of free souls out of the soul of God, and as God thrusts forth his child and veils His own face with ever thicker veils, waiting with infinite restraint for the man to act from within himself in original love, so democratic government must reflect the austerity of God; must break up the solidarity of passion and pelf to the ends of unanimity—the voluntary co-operation of free persons. This austerity of government is in its nature temporary and provisional; its best success is to make itself unnecessary; but while it lasts it is force. It is a fond saying that government derives its just powers from the consent of the governed. Just government exists by the force of the self-governing in repression of the unjust. When the governed consent to justice government will have served its time and can pass into the free and unanimous co-operation of the people.

The Religion of Democracy.

To say that government in America is corrupt is to say that it is soft. It must be steel-fibered if it would get its work done and pass into fraternity. The mob would make it an *alma mater*, a tender providence. And so we are ruled by sentimentality and the stomach —which is plutocracy.

VIII.—So long as the shibboleths of democracy are on every tongue, rich men cannot command the mass of the people in their own persons as rich men, surrounded as they are by the externals of luxury and privilege. If they rule they must do it by deputy. The necessary form of plutocracy is the rule of a supreme good fellow—a boss. The deputy must stand close to the majority and greet the children in the street. There must be in him a mixture of shrewdness and simplicity—shrewdness to follow, with unerring instinct of profit, the intricate lines of a thousand interests and simplicity that he may seem even to himself a kind of great-heart Robin Hood mulcting the rich for the sake of the poor, whereas his real office is the opposite of that.

The government is corrupt because the people are thralled in the traditional sentiment of governmental sovereignty. It is because they try

The Religion of Democracy.

to make the State a nourishing mother—which in the nature of things it cannot be—that it becomes instead a sort of vampire. The people would get justice if they loved justice; it is because they love privilege that they are plundered. The government is cruel and violent because it is weak and sentimental. We have called in the police to compel each other to do good, and so we are bullied with bludgeons. It is necessary to discredit the political theories of Caius Gracchus, to abolish the public circuses and the bread dole, in order that the people may not starve.

The only hope of municipal or other governmental reform is that the people shall come to believe in God and to hate and destroy privilege. But the people will not submit to be rebuked for their love of privilege by pampered men and representatives of a caste.

Crusades by scribes and doctors against the publicans and harlots, the gilded league of scholars in politics listed in bustling combat against the Prince of the Power of the Air—these things make passing contribution to the general fund of humor, but they do not help the people to refrain themselves or to believe in God.

The Religion of Democracy.

IX.—Tragic comedy of the Tagal trench! On one side stand the valiant little brown men, newly wakened, starting up out of ages of sleep, bearing stubborn, formidable arms to defend the Natural Rights of Men and the resounding principles of the French Revolution a century behind the clock! On the other side thirty thousand, and ever more and more, ingenuous boys out of Yankeedom, suckled in these same theories and bred manfully up in the willful gospel of pick-and-choose, are shooting in a grim, nonchalant, disengaged way—not because they approve the action, but because of supposed irresistible, divine decrees uttered out of some Rocky Mountain Horeb. In the background are a great many rapt patriots in prayer, not a few marketmen and promoters, pressing for the interests of civilization—and an English poet singing psalms. Still farther in the background in clear air, stand a million men or so who do not wholly misunderstand. These are tracing out a thesis fraught with amazement and discomfiture for the conservative and complacent classes who make war for the extension of commerce and the enlargement of property rights.

The thesis is that since it is to be admitted that God did not give the Philippine Islands to

The Religion of Democracy.

the Filipinos, to the exclusion of the general interests of the human race, so also it is to be asserted that all material possessions, even in Europe and America, are held subject to the like considerations. It is coming to light in an unexpected way that property is not the datum and foundation of society but the institution and creature thereof. It appears that the whole earth and the seas belong not to the rich, to the capable or the legitimate, but to men, to humanity, and that the supreme source of human law is not nature or necessity, but a certain sublime, sweet reasonableness wherein alone it is possible for individuals to escape from their awful isolation and to meet and understand one another.

The nineteenth century has wrought for the rights of property and the sovereignty of states. Its grand preoccupation has been the attempt to define the individual soul in material terms, to draw in the dust with a firm finger a sacred cincture around a Person. The transcendental sovereignty of State and the Sinaitic sacredness of property are pious inventions made in the interest of this mathematical definition of the soul—there was need of a Firm Finger, and of Indelible Dust! The twentieth century is to disclose the individual in his

The Religion of Democracy.

original and eternal franchise. It will be seen that liberty does not rise up out of the ground, but is born from above; that it is not derived from a definition, and does not depend upon stage machinery.

The Tagal trench is the last ditch of doctrinaire democracy—the fainting century sinks down here on the edge of the utmost West. Here the empire of property plunges to the verge. This tangle of contradictions at the place where the sun both ends and begins his course is the interrogation mark with which the passing century punctuates its period. The twentieth century must answer with the proclamation of a new affirmative.

Over against the rights of property and the sovereignty of nationalities, the new century will proclaim the rights and sovereignty of the soul. There are no natural rights of men that can stand against the spiritual rights of men. It shall be shown that property does not exist in the nature of things; that no man can own anything by mere natural rights—no, not his own body. That property is authentically an attribute of the regenerate, creative soul, and that the only good title is one written in furtherance of the eternal equality and justice.

In the negation of all natural rights, the

The Religion of Democracy.

Right is disclosed; in the denial of every definition of liberty, liberty breaks its bonds and enters into its infinite franchisement, and out of the unmeasured assertion of a man's obligation to universal society for the very texture and quality of his flesh and bones, is born the sovereign, individual souL

CHAPTER VII.

THE WORLD OF NEWS.

I.—THE evangel of democracy shall convince the people of the independence and self-government of God. The slavishness of the world has made it hard to believe that God is free; and the proclamation of the freedom of God shall be the enfranchisement of the people.

It is a servile kind of science—the science of lawyers and pedagogues—that makes God subject to laws; who, then, is the God of God? Let us worship *Him!*

The final guarantee of liberty is the assurance in the people that the government of the soul is of the soul and for the soul. The deepest thing in the religion of democracy is the belief in the universality of the miraculous. The defect of the miracle theories of the old *régime* is that they are aristocratic; they make miracles a privilege and a monopoly, and God a kind of Stuart king breaking the constitution

The Religion of Democracy.

for the pleasure of his courtiers and the confusion of the commons. In their assertion of liberty they do not go far enough to amount to more than mutiny and whim. They show the traditional miracles as flashes of light that serve but to make the darkness felt. If God has only *so* much of liberty, then Fate is strong indeed.

The modern world claims the miraculous on an infinitely greater scale. The progress of modern science is the confusion of all the accepted classifications and the abrogation of all the established laws. It is perceived that everything in nature runs and flows. There is no such thing as finished formulas, and every discovery is held open for revision. It is only the sciolist that would say a last word. The progress of science is the repeal of ecclesastical dogma, because it is the repeal of all dogma— the dogma of physics as of metaphysics.

Out of the widening experience and research one persuasion grows and strengthens, rising into a song of revelation and a profession of faith. It is discovered that everything is reasonable, that everything has relation to every other thing, that everywhere is rhythm, and measure, that the world answers back to the unity of the mind, and is sane.

The Religion of Democracy.

You will not say as a man of science that gravitation will remain to-morrow just what it is to-day, but only that you are persuaded that if God changes *that* he will change everything else in proportion. And doubtless, if the soul of a child should stand in the way the planets would pause and gravitation would turn out. God will have a care that the mill shall grind only ashes and bones.

II.—The happiness of the age is the discovery that this is a world in which there is news. What pedant shall say that the laws of the universe are now just what they were in the former age of steam, or when the ichthyosaurus paddled the secondary seas? Who knows anything about that? It is an extremely improbable surmise obviously designed to put God into a corner. It is prompted by the theological habit which is still strong among us. More likely the laws are different every day—if only to meeken the pedants and freshen the morning. Enough to know that God does not put to intellectual confusion a living man facing the living world.

It is the mournfulest Calvinism to say that the universe of to-day was necessarily involved in that of the day before yesterday, or neces-

The Religion of Democracy.

sarily evolved out of it. The theory of evolution which happens at this moment to be most widespread, should be preached only with a snuffle, or in a Genevan gown. The logic of fatalism is despotism; left to itself the current dogma of predestinarian evolution would balk the hope of democracy and destroy the liberties of the earth. But it is not left to itself; the spirit of the age protests.

The exaltation of the modern spirit is in the assurance that there is always a better world at hand. The axioms of yesterday are not the axioms of to-day. At last it becomes possible to believe in the utter effacement of an evil and the forgiveness of a sin. The barnacled institutions of society break loose from their moorings and are committed to the very stream of change. We shut the book of statics, and attend only to the dynamic laws, the principles of an illimitable orderliness and beautifulness and the demands of a progressive justice that reaches to the uttermost love. If anybody says: "Let us stop here, this is the final right of the matter," he becomes to-morrow an obstacle and a clog. It is perceived that every truth, the propagation of which is endowed and established is a folly on its face, and necessarily false. Pay as you go, is the principle of health,

The Religion of Democracy.

and if the preaching will not pay its keep, and if nobody stands ready to give money and life for it, then let it rest; it is not true to-day. This year's fruit must be nourished from this year's sap. The charter of every association that shall be other than a hindrance and a discouragement must be worded in the future tense, and the getting together of good people as such is degrading and a public nuisance.

III.—In a world in which the phenomenal life of men is held by so slight a tenure, and is constantly exposed to mishaps and the assaults of enemies, it is impossible for a man to be a minister of justice if he is afraid to die. The world is managed at last by the most fearless, by the people that are most deeply rooted in the substratum of things, and least afraid of accidents. A civilization of exquisite refinement, with all the appliances of wealth and culture, lies at the mercy of the barbarians across the border, if the citizens are more afraid of death than the barbarians are. And a luxurious and skeptical aristocracy is easily brought to confusion by the uprising of a people that believe in God. The final test as to which of two things shall remain standing and which shall fall, is which can offer the more

The Religion of Democracy.

martyrs—for which do men in greater numbers stand ready to give their lives?

The conventional statement of the case is that the world is ruled by force, which is true enough in a way; but it is equally and more especially true that the world is ruled by faith. For the power behind the throne of force is fearlessness—which is faith described by a negation.

The universe does not drift aimless, and the great issues are not settled wrong. If the barbarians conquered Rome, it was because there was more faith and fearlessness in Goth and Vandal than there was on the other side; and because the coarsest kind of faith seems to be worth more to the general uses than the finest kind of satire. In the long run the economy of the world is an economy of courage, and the heaviest battalions are heaviest because they are willingest to die. In their origin aristocracies have generally owed their power to their pluck, and they have kept their places as long as they have been more ready than the majority to put their lives in pawn—but not much longer.

Civilization finds its life in losing it. Its organs do their work well in the degree in which they take the eternal for granted and are

The Religion of Democracy.

moved by fearlessness of death and disregard of the inevitable risks and losses. The harmony and grandeur of material structure, the common conveniences, the elegance of living and the charm of civic beauty, these it appears can be got not by a soft and sensuous people rapt in the pursuit of happiness, but only by a people of blood and iron, whose happiness does not depend upon their conveniences, and who do not shrink from death.

It thus becomes evident that the groundwork of civilization is in the unseen, and that the Master-builder of the City of Justice is Fearlessness of Death.

This fearlessness is the beginning of science and art. It makes the engines of manufacture and war; it can plow, build ships and railroads, and plan new social constitutions. It is the awe and majesty of human life—the mystery and the magnificence; it makes and supersedes the rituals of all religions, and it creates the great poems and pictures.

IV.—From this standpoint it is seen that neither Rome nor any other sectarian church is qualified to set up that universal spiritual power that is to exalt the world. The faith that can furnish the energy of such an enterprise must be of

The Religion of Democracy.

the elemental kind, the faith of warriors, artists and explorers, the faith of laborers and of illiterate and primitive men, the faith of Jesus—and of children.

The work of the Church in the days of its indispensable usefulness, its moral glory, was to bring this brooding, latent faith to clear and deliberate consciousness, that it might know itself and comprehend its destiny· and that it might, in the maturity of strenth, grapple with the faithlessness, the moral cowardice, of the antique civilizations and put them to perpetual shame.

The drift of antiquity was to put death out of sight, and to degrade that elemental faith that is exercised in fearlessness of death. It sophisticated the primary life-issues and obscured the significance of the primary facts of existence, as that one must labor and that one must die. The antique world did not very seriously occupy itself with social reforms or the practical achievement of justice, though its literature teems with classics of Utopian speculation. Its passion was to escape from the world of death and labor into a realm of harmony and justice that was all too exclusively ideal.

Over against this futile aspiration the Church raised up a working faith. But the

The Religion of Democracy.

Child of the Church was greater than its foster-mother; the Church could not itself fulfill the promise of its faith. The ground plan of the Church was not grand enough to contain and accomplish that conscious, catholic faith whose root is in the elemental trustfulness of a barbarian or a child, and whose fulfillment is universal, social revolution and the establishment of civilization upon new and spiritual foundations. The Church was incapable of such an achievement because its framework, its polity, cultus and discipline were wrought and elaborated in contravention of the primordial principle of faith. Catholicism, as an institution and system, was irreconcilable with Catholicism as a moral ideal and a world-reforming purpose—for the sufficient reason that the institution and system were made of the stuff of the old world that so needed to be reformed. The cultus and dogma of Catholicism were an outcome of Greek culture and Roman law; the system was conceived and worked out under the influences that had created, and that continued to permeate the old world secular society, which were in a general sense derived from the idea that a man must make the most of himself—the idea in fine of the self-made man.

The scheme of Catholicism furnished a sys-

The Religion of Democracy.

tem of delicate devices for improving and purifying one's own soul and reaching up to God. It was grounded in the prepossession that the divinest attitude of the human spirit is as of one that stands tiptoe on the earth with hands and eyes strained upward to a diviner world—which was also the prepossession of Greek culture. Catholicism could not conquer or comprehend the earth because of its profound moral abstraction; its aim was not directed toward the earth, but toward heaven. Its strained effort to attain to the ideal became a corruption and scandal in the flesh, and an apostacy from that elemental faith of plain men, which takes God for granted and goes forth to set things right upon the earth.

V.—In the Renaissance, the naive faith of primitive Christianity became conscious that the ecclesiastical cultus was an obstacle. The essential faith of the Church made ready to break its barriers and to undertake the radical conversion of the society and the conquest of the world. Faith was quickened into self-consciousness by the antagonism of its opposites, and rose up into the strength of the modern spirit. The revival of letters was not a return to Greece, but a conversion of Greek learning

The Religion of Democracy.

to the uses of faith and to the ends of a modern civilization which claims all history and achievement, and rejoices in all, and whose fraternity reaches back.

The characteristic attitude of the faith of modernity is that of one with firm-set feet and forth-right eyes intent upon the beautilessness of the world. Religion is ceasing to be thought of as an aspiration after the divine, and is coming to be nothing but sheer trust in God despite all difficulties, a conception that seems both primitive and unsophisticated, and also final and scientific. The cultus of the churches, their casuistries and spiritual calisthenics, their elaborate means of grace and their striving, rapturous prayers are of the old world—Hellenic, without the measure and sincerity of the Greek, and Hebraic without the sobriety and realism of the Jew. They are the old world minus what made the old world livable. The spring of their intricate perversions is the feeling that something — anything — everything must be done to find out what the will of God is; whereas the desire of God through the ages seems to be that a man should come at length to have a reasonable will of his own. This is an idea that seems hardly to have dawned upon the ecclesiastical mind, although the life of the

The Religion of Democracy.

secular world is aglow with the feeling that liberty is a reality, that a living man can conceive and execute designs that contain an element of utter and absolute originality, and that God will back up a good plan, even though he may not have furnished, and indeed would not furnish the specifications in advance.

The consciousness of freedom grows apace. It is no longer possible to believe that God is the author of the confusions of history or the fearful iniquities of social institutions. We perceive that we are jointly responsible with Him for the present condition of the universe. It appears that the providence of God is limited to making the best of every emergency so far as may be done consistently with the liberty and responsibility of men. And it by no means follows that He established the existing churches, states, law-codes, and commercial customs because they exist.

Not only is it true that the world as it stands to-day is not a theocracy, but it appears that theocracy is not a thing to be desired—that God will not have it so. The revelation of history and of all experience is that God will not reign over the people, but has set His heart upon it that through faith in Him the people shall reign over themselves.

The Religion of Democracy.

The beginning of history is in theocracy; but democracy is the consummation. And all the intermediate stages of confusion and bewilderment, of misery and disappointment, are, it would seem, better in the eyes of God, and more desirable than the sway of unquestioned goodness, and the smooth obedience of a puppet world.

VI.—The reasonable object of devotion is disclosed not as a thing recondite and obscure, but as the most obvious thing and what might have been expected. The business of a man is to carve into the substance of this visible world the most excellent thing that—in the face of the scanned and sifted facts—he can clearly think. Probably there is nothing too good for God, and everything is plastic to fine art and reform. Though stupidity and fear beset the path with difficulties, and make it bristle with menace, still it is reasonable to insist that the thing most practical is that which is most humane, most exalted and most just. It is hard to reform a jail without getting into it, or to take off a tea tax without a revolution; there is an inertia of well-meaning dullness that seems like fatality —like the slow crunching of a traveler's bones in the crack of a glacier.

The Religion of Democracy.

But the traveler journeys on, for the traveler is the soul.

VII.—It is a superficial judgment that this is a sordid and God-forgetting age, because it is occupied with questions of board and clothes, and bent upon getting them settled right. If the people were sordid and had lost faith in the eternal justice, they would not risk their half loaf on the dangerous chance of getting a whole one. It has been finely said that a gentleman is one who stands ready to lay down his life for little things, and that is the temper of democracy.

If the people are willing to risk everything for the sake of a circumstance, it is because they have an unformulated faith in the reality of those everlasting arms that sustain defeated causes. The feeling that is abroad that one may afford the luxury of living and dying for a decency, comes of a perception, more or less clear, that this visible flow of things is a kind of hieroglyph of an eternal order, and that justice and beauty written in this wax are somehow graven in an adamant, and so are worth while.

It becomes an impertinence to expatiate upon the misery of the poor—implying that an evil thing might stand if only it were not intolera-

The Religion of Democracy.

ble. The right moment of reform does not fall at the limit of endurance. We will not be ruled by sheer, infidel necessity; it is enough that the thing is wrong.

It is the greatness of the age that it is engrossed in economics; that it sees in tangible things wrought by the labor of men, sacramental values, and the materials of religion. This is the beginning of a new order of things more beautiful and joyous than has yet been seen on the earth; for how was it possible to make the earth glorious while the poets and artists stood gazing into heaven? Now at length, after thousands of years of wistful longings for another world, there is hope that we may accept the situation and take time to put the earth in order. It is not because this earth is all, but because it is not all, and we can afford to be liberal, and because democracy has found a standing ground in the eternal from which it can exert a tremendous leverage upon all the old social snags.

To bring justice and beauty upon the earth in wisdom, freedom and fearlessness of death, that is the whole ritual and service of the religion of the incarnation. Its theology is that a man is a son of God, and that his work is worldmaking as God's work is.

The Religion of Democracy.

VIII.—That spiritual power—independent and universal—which was the longing of the Middle Ages, shall fulfill itself in the sovereignty of the peoples of the world, focused in the heart of that people which has most of faith in God, and is most magnanimous for justice. This is the plain vocation of the people of the United States; there is to-day on the earth no other people that can exemplify on a grand and convincing scale the spiritual and sacrificial principle of popular sovereignty.

It is said that the road of territorial extension and governmental aggrandizement would be a new departure for the American people; but that is only superficially and technically true. That road is a smooth, easy declivity, trodden hard by all the world before us, a road with whose trend we are ourselves, after all, sufficiently familiar. The ideals that make for bigness of government and vastness of territory are the air we have breathed for a generation; the matter of the exact frontier limit is a matter of detail, mainly interesting from the point of view of professional politics and traditional consistency. If the old ideals were to continue with us, it would be unimportant whether or not they should be applied to another island or two. The rise and fall of nations is in the rise

The Religion of Democracy.

and fall of the spirit that actuates them, and is little affected by accidents of polity.

The matter of supreme interest to universal history is whether America, having come to the parting of the ways, shall choose according to the old world fatality, the greatness of a government, and the expanded egotism of patriotic pride or shall choose in unprecedented self-denial the freedom of the peoples beyond her boundaries. The latter way, and not the way of a greater government, is a new departure —a way fresh with the dew of the world's morning, trodden by many persons from time to time, but never yet by a people.

The choice is exigent. We cannot pause at the parting of the ways and decide against both alternatives. In the laws of morality everything moves for better or worse. To settle back as we were is the one thing utterly impossible. The test that is to be required of the nation that would be the leading spirit in the moral empire of democracy is that it shall be willing to seem less in order that other peoples may be more.

The rise of democracy as a universal spiritual power would follow upon the rise of a nation disinterestedly devoted to the cause of liberty, a nation that should escape from itself, as no nation has yet done, and live out into the world. The basis of self-government at last is simply self-denial, and the universal spiritual power would be established on the day that a great nation should set its face steadfastly toward the City of Sacrificial Love.

But democracy is greater than any nation; it may be balked, delayed, defeated; but it is unconquerable. The very life of the modern world is in it, and though to-day only the children should understand its secret it would certainly prevail.

It may be that the nation which is to be the master spirit must be gathered out of the whole family of nations — a kinship of justice and equality, a comradeship whose hands reach round the world.

The states grow hard and brittle, and the earth grows small. The *orbis terrarum* bounded by the equator to-day is smaller and easier to compass than it was when it surrounded only the Mediterranean lake. The difficulty is *not* to compass it. When the whole earth pays tribute to one's daily meals it is hard to keep up the parochial illusions. The endeavor to consider the affairs of one country without reference to the affairs of other countries becomes a labored abstraction, and a kind of trifling.

Certainly there is not a fence in the world

The Religion of Democracy.

that will stand much pressure. Commerce is on the side of universal democracy, and it is irresistible in the long run, and will not mind a custom or a prejudice any more than the tide will mind a king. By and by, after the boundaries have ceased to serve the money-lords and men of bonds, who dominate the councils of what is called the Concert of Powers, these will pool their interests and wipe out all the frontiers—unless the people shall have arrived before them, and destroyed the boundaries for other purposes. Everywhere the hearts of the people are aching with the expectation of release and liberty; the way is prepared for the apostolate of the religion of democracy; it cannot be long before its priestless temples shall rise.

IX.—It is not that we are to look forward to a finished and perfect social order. Perfection is a hope that all nature exists to discourage; and the charm of a beautiful thing or of a just deed is that it is of infinite suggestion and easily transcends itself—leading one on and on.

What may be said of the religion of the incarnation is not that it will change the world to happiness in a day, but that it will defeat the tendency to collapse and draw the world out of that endless, desperate cycle of glory and decay

The Religion of Democracy.

which hitherto has claimed the nations like a fate, and tumbled all the cloud-piercing Babel-towers in the dust; and that it will lay indestructible foundations for a civilization of immeasurable and endless improvement.

The death of nations is in morbid ideality, an ideality that feeds upon itself and forgets to live. The aristocracies perish because they become self-cultivating and cease to be creative, and the governments are overthrown because they dream of empire and neglect the common, economic facts.

The religions of the world in general have afforded no availing remedy for this bathos of history, this chronic tendency to anticlimax, but have often tended rather to precipitate disaster. At times they have seemed to infect the earth like virulent diseases, because they have spent themselves in stimulating their devotees in spiritual culture and have despised art and reform. The unanimous persuasion of the spiritual specialists of every age and country that God is all in all, and is therefore exclusively responsible for things as they are, has been the assurance of the fatalism of the privileged classes, and has done more than the lusts of the flesh to discourage repentance and prepare the great social calamities.

The Religion of Democracy.

To be sure it has been the usual teaching of these specialists that religion includes ethics and requires that a man shall do right. But since this right has been systematically distinguished from the mere candid promptings of an unsophisticated mind, and has always been referred back to the will of God; and since the will of God is, by the premises, mainly to be gathered from the established order, it becomes difficult to escape from the vicious circle, and difficult to find in what goes by the name of ethics a standing ground from which to execute reform.

Conceivably the world might have escaped from this fatal round by the use of prayer. It might have been God's way to furnish to such as should apply, specific intimations and detailed designs of what a man should do—or he might at least have provided the priests with such patterns, to be by them given out in piecework to the faithful. Men have had such hopes; church polities have been built upon them, and doubtless there are many pious people that expect their daily messages, and perhaps receive them. Yet it is evident that, in general, the sanest saints do not expect them, and that for the ordinary run of things God does not furnish men with diagrams of duty. It is clear that, in

The Religion of Democracy.

the main, He has thrown the world upon its own conscience, and that He is not, and will not be, all in all.

Of course the vast perversions of religion are not to be attributed wholly, or even principally, to the priests; and it is to be borne in mind that even in the most perverted religions there has always been an unpriestly element of simple love and joy, and the desire for what is beautiful. But the general account of all the priestly establishments, so far as they have been priestly, is that they have been the institutionalizations of the faithlessness of men, in view of the practical difficulties of living.

At their best they have furnished consolations for the lack of faith, and at their worst they have provided systematic devices for doing away with the felt need of it. If one would but believe something a little hard to credit, or do something a little hard to do, accept a creed, burn an offering or buy an indulgance, nothing else should be required and the sacrifice should be accounted faith.

The theory that a man may save his soul by accepting an incomprehensible proposition in divinity is not Protestantism, but a poisoning of the wells of Protestantism. And scarcely since the world began has orthodoxy for one

The Religion of Democracy.

moment made common cause with faith, or struck with her a single venturesome blow for love and justice.

X.—Over against the rabble and jargon of what are called the religious faiths, democracy lifts up its voice for faith. The faiths with their stubborn theologies, their forbidding sacraments and their special unctions, are convicted of intellectual vanity and spiritual pride; they build partition walls, foment discords, and excommunicate souls; but faith excludes no one. Faith can transcend all the boundaries of races, nations, classes, sects, and find terms of expression for the oneness of human interests —the vast orderliness of the moral universe.

XI.—Pass around the world at night over the sleeping cities and the wide, silent lands—New York, Chicago, Pekin, Calcutta, Paris, the farms, the innumerable dwellings scattered over the steppes and prairies; note the pause and suspense, the prostration of myriads of souls. This is the immemorial common prayer, the oldest ritual of faith, the original and universal sacrament. Dreams are the distemper of sleep, but the subconscious deeps of it are, it would seem, the recuperation of faith and the intimacy of God. Out of sleep the timeless man comes forth into time to accomplish the incarnation. The program of valiant enterprise is to do what seems good in the morning, and the perfection of faith is an utter confidence in the resources that are withdrawn behind the veil of sleep and death.

The illusion of culture and pride is that sleep is the weakness and death the overthrow of life; but the discovery of humility and faith is that sleep and death are the ground in which life grows.

Day by day, sunward, in vast procession— yet each going alone—the millions of the world pass through the gates of sleep into the universal sanctuary. Herein is a catholic communion without schism, under this serene dome are no divisions of interest.

Day by day, a universal spiritual concord is typed in the unanimity of deep, dispassionate sleep. The day comes and the day's work is to press upon the striving, conscious world, the fulfillment of this prophecy, to cast into concrete images, wrought in the stuff of nature, the cool, sane promptings of receptive sleep.

CHAPTER VIII.

THE CASTE OF GOODNESS.

I.—THE modern man is standing at a point of view from which it would seem to be possible for the simplest to see that the dream of the youth of Lamennais, the dream of Pope Leo XIII., is indeed a dream. Democracy cannot make terms with any kind of ecclesiastical trust or spiritual monopoly. The life of Lamennais is a tragic demonstration of this impossibility as his "Book of the People" and "Words of a Believer" are among the earliest disclosures of the spiritual meaning of democracy.

It is said in Europe that the Pope has canonized democracy, but it is a one-sided wooing; democracy will never canonize the Pope. Yet it salutes in him the most consistent representative of the old *régime*—the hero of the dying world.

The Roman Church as an institution and reasoned system antagonizes at every point the

The Religion of Democracy.

witness of the modern spirit. Rome is fatalist, skeptic and pessimist clear through—except for glorious miracles. Modernity, with its matter-of-fact assurance that a man does really choose his way and achieve his own designs, its confidence in the possibility of science and its fixed persuasion that it is a good thing to be alive on any terms whatever, turns away from Rome with a shrug, and does not stop to argue. As for the multitudinous Protestant and sectarian churches they are things of incredible mystification, having but one aspect in common—a genius for compromise and self-contradiction. It is true that the inner spirit of Protestantism is nothing other than the modern spirit; but Protestant ecclesiasticism as it stands is a jungle of impossibilities—a disastrous attempt to put new wine into old bottles. Protestantism has shone clear and illustrious only in those times when for a moment it has forgotten its corporate privileges and launched itself boldly into the secular world—as in the rise of the Dutch Republic, or the planting of the New England colonies. For the destruction of spiritual monopolies is the logic of Protestantism, whereunto it is pressed by an irresistible necessity.

The Religion of Democracy.

II.—The mediæval Church is the placenta of the modern world. It has been indispensable to the generation of the new social order, but it becomes noisome and an offence with the birth of the modern and spiritual conception of secular society. Within the body of the Roman Empire, whose law was fatalism, skepticism and pessimism reduced to system and statute, the ancient Church was formed—out of Roman and imperial materials, to hold the germ of modernity—the principle that a man may be the son of God.

Back of the blank negations of the Roman civilization there lay a long history of moral discomfiture. Rome was the ordered embodiment of the disappointment of Greek liberty and culture—the stubborn desperation of the self-made man. It is to be noted that Greek liberty could stand without self-contradiction or a qualm, face to face with chattel slavery, modern liberty cannot do that. This marks a world-wide distinction between two different things. The ground of the former was in temporal circumstances, the ground of the latter is in the eternal constitution of the soul. Liberty to the Greek was an accomplishment; to the modern man it is a primordial right. There is a Stoic saying that a brave man is in a way

The Religion of Democracy.

superior to God, for God owes it to his mere nature that He is not afraid, but man to his own achievement. Such a saying might stand as a symbol of the top-loftiness, the moral giddiness and the predestined failure of that liberty and culture of Greece upon the ruin of which Rome laid out her flinty roads, and deployed her legions.

Rome had settled it that after all a man was but a man—*chair a plaisir et chair a canon.* But in the body of this death and discouragement, the Roman Church was a thing formed out of the substance of the dying to gestate the soul of the modern world. For the soul of the modern world is the idea of liberty, not as something to be accomplished at the end of life, but something to be claimed in the beginning, despite adverse possessions and every vested interest—the idea of inalienable rights and the mystery and awe of a co-creatorship with God, and a joint responsibility. The Church was the stuff of the old social *régime* impregnated with the miracle of the divinity of a man—a marvel which contains the promise and prophecy of that universality of the miraculous, or universality of moral freedom, which is the religion of democracy and in the realization of which both the old social order and the ancient Church are now to pass away.

The Religion of Democracy.

That the Church in its historical conception cannot be the embodiment of the Holy Spirit of Emancipation or its perpetual vehicle, that it is, and must be in the nature of things only a scaffolding destined to be destroyed, grows day by day more evident. The vertigo and motor-paralysis of the Protestant churches, their inability to move, even by the smallest advances toward that church-unity, 'for which they so unanimously pray—this spectacle is the final exhibit of the proof that Protestantism and the Protestant churches are contradictory terms. The only unity, of any hope or any value, is to be sought out in the open air of common secularity. The sectarian church that would be most forward to the goal of the unity and company of faithful men, must make *auto-da-fé* of everything that makes it a spiritually privileged corporation must strive, and be shriven of every note and character, of every habit of mind and posture of soul that belongs to the caste of goodness and the tradition of a dying world. Into the fire of the sacrifice must go not only the hierarchical pretensions, and the fond imaginations of sacramentalism, but also the *caput mortum* of Hellenic theology, the intellectual vagaries of liberalism, and a thousand other ancient follies and clerical conceits; for all

The Religion of Democracy.

these things are of the body, and quality of the ancient Church, and must pass with the passing of the old world to which that Church belongs.

III.—The Church as it stands to-day is not merely a cumberer of the ground; it is an obstacle to faith, and a preventer of goodness. Its smoking lamps make the darkness murky, and its weakness and incompetency grow to what is worse. It obscures the spiritual aim of democracy, reduces liberty to a sentiment, and equality and fraternity to an affected fellowship, or a mutual benefit. Its envious and paltry divisions thwart the hope of social unanimity; it precipitates a crystallization of society in terms of emotion, intellect and taste, and so scatters the conscience and paralyzes the will.

The Church was the bearer of faith only so long as it remained inknit in the very body and texture of the old secular society. When faith grew up out of the old world and took the field in the struggle for civil liberty, it was commissioned to become the informing and all-penetrating power of a new world, and there was no longer any moral meaning in the ancient ecclesiastical system. It served only to encyst the principle of faith and keep it out of the gen-

The Religion of Democracy.

eral circulation. The Church became a rival and a hindrance to the spiritual commonwealth.

Before that broadening of the horizon that came with the Renaissance and the Reformation, the Church's ordered scheme of special miracles shone as an open rift in the black dome of fate that had settled down upon the ancient world. The miracles of the Church were a standing witness to the liberty of the spirit in the midst of a world of immutable and cruel law. Its very superstitions and excesses were as a corrosion of the hard armor of the old fatalism, skepticism and pessimism, and there was no anchorite, or cenobite, no pilgrim or palmer, that did not pay tribute to the modern world, and serve the cause of liberty. But the time came when the Christian program, as represented by the Church, became no longer credible. Its stubborn assertion of an outworn theory became a denial of conceptions that were infinitely more inspiring as they were more easy to understand. A profounder moral experience and a larger synthesis brought men to a pass where they must either conceive the whole world as instinct with miraculous freedom, or else must altogether deny the possibilty of freedom and sink back into the old despair. The

The Religion of Democracy.

arrival at this juncture was the signal for what is called the Reformation, which should have been much more than a reformation, and would have been if the reformers had believed a little more in their mission and kept close to their inspirations. The plain logic of "private judgment" and "justification by faith" was the complete discrediting of all established spiritual oracles and the effacement of the ancient corporate Church. If the old Church system was only corrupt and needed healing, the Reformation was the greatest crime in history, and the reformers were indeed, as the Roman historians say, very devils of discord. The Reformation is justified only as being in spirit and intent a revolution and the putting away of a dead thing. The social convulsions that followed, the moral welter and confusion, the age-long harassment of sectarian rivalries, the fierce, intestine wars, the brooding pestilence of cant and the belittling of God—these things came of the Reformation, not because it was wrong but because it was not thorough; it left the people still looking for a privileged corporation. The new presbyters were the old priests, after all, and their affirmation of the lesser creed became the denial of the greater. The faith of the Protestant churches mocked

The Religion of Democracy.

the faith of the modern world. For more than four hundred years they have been minimizing their professions, with the fission of their bodies, until now they are incredible because they claim so little. Their demands upon the confidence of men have reached the most tenuous extreme. Their faith verges to infidelity, and the people turn doubting from their altars to cheer in the streets the name of Jesus.

IV.—The simple truth is that the churches are in danger of forgetting the very meaning of faith. What they now call by that name is for the most part not faith at all. If other than a hereditary prejudice or a social concession, it is a persuasion that comes at the end of an argument, or a feeling that follows an emotional stir. Faith could abide in the Church only so long as it took its church for granted; when the Church became itself an object of faith, faith was turned to a philosophy, or an infatuation. When the Church ceased to be in some sense coterminous with secular society, it lost the one thing of value that it contained—lost the originality and ingenuousness of faith—lost the kind of faith that forgets itself and removes mountains by intending heart and mind upon the mountains, the faith of the Maid of Orleans

The Religion of Democracy.

and St. Francis of Assisi, which is precisely the most modern and democratic kind. The faith of a sectarian church—in which description Rome, as represented in the modern world, must certainly be included—is but the ritual of a cult, the shibboleth of a pious caste, or the philosophy of a school.

The faith that is an adventure of the soul, and an originating moral energy can get no gain or succor from the sectarian churches. The genetic kind of faith which is the very breath of the modern spirit, which is the spring of science and of humanizing enterprise, which believes in spite of doubt, that this unintelligible world is at bottom reasonable, confronting the antagonisms of classes and nations with a fixed assurance that there is a justice that is best for all, making the strong the willing slaves of the weak, and convincing the people of the equality of souls—the faith that is preparing the triumph of democracy, creating a new and inspiring literature and clearing the way for a commerce that shall claim the markets for the man—this faith is not bred in sectarian churches.

And no reform of the sects will avail to produce such faith, no revival of their spirits, no purification, disinfection or purgation. The

The Religion of Democracy.

quickening of the desire to improve their spiritual condition would but intensify the evil. It is necessary to unchurch the churches before they can serve the common cause of souls. Their existence is a contradiction, and their safety is to turn against themeslves.

The Religion of Democracy.

CHAPTER IX.

THE RISE OF A DEMOCRATIC CATHOLIC CHURCH.

I.—The religious trusts are bankrupt, and the caste of goodness and truth is ripe for dissolution; but the Church in its original charter rises to the emergency of the world. The societies founded in particularism, exclusion and monopoly give place to a Catholic Church founded in the universal and the eternal, and in the essential and permanent characteristics of the human spirit. The churches of the past have been only types and symbols foreshowing—sometimes in glorious and inspiring parable, sometimes in distorted and monstrous caricature — the Church catholic and democratic which is to comprehend the design of the universal spiritual revolution and establish the people in the beginnings of liberty. It has taken nearly nineteen hundred years for a catholic church to become a possibility.

Catholicism is the taking in of the last man

The Religion of Democracy.

with confidence that for him, too, as well as for the rest, life has meaning and is reasonable; it is the taking in of the whole cosmos with confidence that it is all of one piece and hangs together to the last detail; it is the taking in of every human interest of body and soul in faith that the base and servile can be subdued to liberty, art and joy, and finally it is the embracing of all the ages in the belief that they have mutual and independent significance and a cumulative purpose. One has but to turn the pages of history with the most casual hand to perceive that the conception of such a catholicism was impossible to any of the ages that have gone by; while the most cursory survey of the contemporary world will show that such a catholicism is both the passion and the conviction of the age in which we live.

The Church that is in the making transcends every human device and institution; its establishment is not in the imagination and invention of men, but in the reality and persistence of God. The Churches of the past have generally professed a superhuman constitution. But it is evident that they have, without exception, sprung out of limited and mortal ideas, since they have scattered the people, rejected or ignored the expanding vision of the world, sepa-

The Religion of Democracy.

rated the sacred from the secular, and broken the continuity of the ages. At last, after many failures of pride and the discrediting of innumerable theories, the divine and royal humility is compelling its lesson upon the hearts of men. There will arise a Church that is not the product of a theory, but that grows out of the living presence of God—resting not upon special revelations or particular ideas, but upon the axioms of faith.

The Churches of the past might conceivably have been the inventions of priests and princes; it is possible to imagine that they might have existed even though there were no God. But the Church of the modern expectation is frankly impossible if there be no God. It is possible for men to get together on the basis of a sacramental theory or a proposition in divinity, whether the theory or the proposition be true or false; but it is not possible for men to get together on the ground of the eternal reasonableness and justice, unless indeed there be an eternal Reasonableness and Justice to whom they all alike have access. The religion of democracy is effacing the guide-lines and diagrams of traditional authority, committing to oblivion the ground plans of the ancient Churches. Therein it in-

The Religion of Democracy.

curs a fearful and magnificent risk. If God does not exist, the result of it all can be only weltering anarchy and the ruin of the world. On the other hand, if God be real, we shall now behold unveiled the demonstration of His undeniable glory.

II. The ecclesiology of a democratic catholicism is the ultimate form of social organization. The Church is to stand as the ecumenical democracy, the international republic of humanity in the day when the superstition of State sovereignty shall become incredible and the huge, meaningless political aggregates shall lose their strength. The strength of the wrangling empires is in their mutual jealousy and fear—a relic of the feudal tradition and the old ethnic isolation. Commerce and communication are steadily relaxing the sinews of international war. Already the profounder antagonisms are not those that separate nations, but those that separate classes. Men are drawn together in these days not by the blood-bond, but by unanimity in ideals; as the new social order is born not of the flesh but of the spirit. The hulks of empire may rot by the sea for a time, but the life and motion will go out of them with the rise of the tide of catholic democracy.

The Religion of Democracy.

The Church is the people organized in liberty. Its motive and design is the constitution of a universal society in unconstrained equality, the creation of a world-wide civilization in the spirit of art—in a word, it is the realization in the flesh of the Eternal Life. Surely, in such an enterprise the sword of State must bear a subordinate and diminishing part.

The law of the State is static; it is merely provisional and conservative—it is not fit for art or for any high and venturesome enterprise or endeavor. Half the cruelties of history have come of a monstrous and abnormal knight-errantry of governments. The sword is good for pruning, but it cannot make things grow.

The State is the disciplinary arm of the Church; regarded as an end in itself, or as an object of devotion, it is an imposture and a delusion. The use of government is to furnish certain of the mechanical and material conditions for the growth of art and the humanities; and this work it can faithfully and effectually do only when it shall be strictly subordinated to the superior and wider social organization representative of the uncompelled ambitions and devotions of the people.

Governments to be strong must be not large but small in extent of territorial jurisdiction.

The Religion of Democracy.

The success and progress of governments in this generation has been mainly limited to municipalities. The ideal and poetic aspiration of the new century will express itself in the creation of splendid and cosmopolitan cities, the soul of which shall be the Universal Church. The tendency of the current of imperialism is to parochialize the universe—to make the whole earth Slav or Saxon, on the pattern of the village commune or the town meeting. The promise of catholicism is the opposite of that. It would universalize the parish, bringing the All of things to bear upon the local and provincial—planting the university at every crossroads.

The Church will have institutions and architecture. It will convert the old cathedrals and build new ones. The great things of mediæval catholicism were for the future; the cathedral that was a forum of public meeting, a gallery of arts, a guildhall of handicrafts, a school of letters, and a possession of everybody—prophesied of democracy. And with the awakening of the European peoples it is certain that those glorious buildings, fallen now into mournful abstraction, shall be reclaimed by the artists and the workers, and redeemed to the living world. It is not less to be expected that

The Religion of Democracy.

the cathedrals of Europe will yield suggestion for other and different fanes and minsters in Western lands, buildings which will be named not for the seat of a bishop, but for the standard of a people—each a pledge of hospitality for all travelers, a shrine and statehouse of democracy and a nerve center of civilization.

III.—All things grow from the seed—nothing is created out of nothing. The future comes out of the past, and the seed is not quickened except it die. The new Church will come out of the old Church, when the seed is ready for the furrow—when a little podded sect stands ready in its heart to die.

Three notes and signs, which characterize—yes, constitute—the existing sects, will characterize and constitute the Church of the future by their unprecedented absence. The three essential notes of a sect are the attempted establishment of the sacred in separation from the secular, of good people in separation from bad people, and of true propositions in separation from false. The rise of the new catholicism is in the dawning conviction that these distinctions, in so far as they are pregnant and fruitful, are self-vindicatory, and do not need to be institutionalized or established. The risk of

The Religion of Democracy.

losing the eternal things in the temporal things, of contaminating the good by the touch of the evil, of missing the reality through too earnest a regard of the phenomenon—this is the intrinsic and inevitable risk of faith, the trial and task of those who would live in the real world and build the City of the Soul. It is the faith of the religion of the Incarnation that the risks are not losses; that it is good to break the barriers and live out dangerously into the world.

The Church shall discover the eternal in the flesh. It shall understand that civilization is the sum of all sacraments and the supreme and most intimate test of the spirits of men. It shall see in the problem of labor and bread the involute of every spiritual and eternal issue. The Church shall engross itself in materials, in the humanities, the courtesies and the arts. It shall work a new orientation of the common law, shifting the legal point of view from property to persons, destroying the fetish of capital and denying the capitalist a hearing save as a member of the fraternity of work.

It shall be disclosed that God has so framed this tangible world that it will respond only to the communion and unanimity of men—balking and confusing all science and art, all labor and commerce save such as is accomplished in love and faith. The building of the world-city will be seen to be the goal of history—unattainable save through mighty regenerations and redemptions. The nations hitherto have been the serfs of nature, *ascirpti glebæ*, thralled and cumbered in the clod. The earth has possessed the people, and history has been mainly a gloss upon economics. The program of the new era is to put the people in possession of the earth— to put the whole people in possession of the whole earth.

So much for the first note of the resurgent Church—its sacred and eternal secularity.

Secondly, the Church will utterly shatter the caste of goodness and definitely abandon the attempt to mark a distinction between good persons and the bad. Its sacraments must be offered to all the humble and child-hearted without any kind of stipulation of conformity or faintest implication of special sanctity. The Church will refuse to exercise what is called spiritual discipline, and it will jealously guard its offices from the imputation of being particularly pious.

For to be particularly pious is not merely pharisaic, it is flat paganism; it savors of the siege of Troy and the platitudes of Greek philosophers; it is flying in the face of Christianity and making the clergy and all the communicants a jest.

According to Christianity, goodness is not a thing for which a man ought to be publicly marked and praised, but a thing for which he should be privately congratulated. Christianity has no economy of certificated virtues; it does not deal in medals and diplomas. It sets up no model, pattern, paragon or celestial fashion-plate. Its ideal goodness is ineffably good because, with unfaltering sweetness and strength, it confounds itself incontinently in the bad.

The Church will regard itself as constitutionally coterminous with secular society. The point is not that the Church will strive to reach the very low and bad people—it has been trying to do that for a long time with curious and confused results; the point is that at last the dead-set to save souls will be abandoned; and instead of keeping up the haggard, weary chase, the Church will simply assume both the pursuers and the pursued—regarding them all alike as equal constituents of the commonwealth of souls.

The religion of democracy takes in all the people without exception, not because it is indifferent to moral and spiritual distinctions,

The Religion of Democracy.

and not because it holds that men are naturally good or even that everybody is sure to be saved. It is not because it makes light of the eternal and tragic issue between Jerusalem and Babylon, but because it would give its whole soul to that issue, that it has written upon its doorposts and the footpace of its altar: Judge not. Unto this last and He was made sin.

And, in the third place, the Church will abandon the attempt to truss up and underpin the Truth, and will, on the contrary, repose in quiet strength upon those sills and girders of the universal frame which have been or hereafter shall be discovered. It will appear that the Truth is not a sacred deposit to be kept in a box under guard of priestly seneschals, but a living, tremendous Thing—able to take care of Itself as well as of all who will trust it. Such is obviously the case with the truth of physics; so it is also with the truth of metaphysics.

If what is called a lie will wear as well as the truth in the long run, it cannot be a lie. The truth at last must be proved in experience; there is after all no other credible proof. That an unbroken succession of mutes, dervishes and fakirs—or of prebendaries, deans and curates—have sworn to a thing for a thousand years is no proof.

The Religion of Democracy.

It is time to take off the handicap from heresy, and to absolve the shackled clergy from their vows. Time was when the idea of the Church as the prop and pillar of the truth was credible enough—perhaps indispensable to the gestation of the modern world. Given the profound philosophical and practical skepticism of ancient society, it was perhaps impossible for the truth of a spiritual democracy to get credit otherwise than as a miracle of special revelation, imposed and guaranteed from without, and neither to be proved nor disproved by ordinary experience. But the rising spirit of Christianity, coming to clear utterance in the Renaissance and the Reformation, and to general acceptance in the subsequent times, has reduced that conception of the Church to hopeless anachronism. It is the faith of the modern world that the common mind, standing over against the common universe, can in hunger and thirst after reasonableness understand somewhat of reality. And it is coming to be perceived by the people that, as a corps of physicians sworn to a particular scheme of therapeutics, would stand convicted of moral and intellectual levity and would be disqualified for the practice of their profession, so the sworn preachers of the churches are disqualified to preach.

The Religion of Democracy.

The preachers seem to be retained in a special interest and mortgaged to the platitudes. The people long for the disengaged accents of an unmuffled man. It is necessary to freely differ from the Apostles in order to recommend the things they stood for. And if the people do not believe that a God may be the son of man or a man the son of God, it is largely because they have been told so only by people who seemed to be obliged to say so.

Most of the clergy are in a difficult case, for they really do believe all the inspiring things that they have promised to believe; they must therefore continue to lie under the imputation that they say what is proper to say. But for the rest the remedy is easy—it had been good for Herod to break his vow and save the life of a prophet.

The attempt to unify the churches by soft diplomacies and compromises, the search for a minimum creed to meet the requirements of the most attenuated mind, the letting go of the facts by which the people must live or die, for the sake of sociability—all this is one of the pitifulest spectacles that these times present.

Dire obstacles to the new catholicism are those amiable clergymen who would trade off the law of gravitation for the sake of getting

The Religion of Democracy.

everybody to agree. Catholicism cannot be got out of compromise. And the new catholicism is simply thoroughgoing Protestantism with all the loyalty to truth and the devotion to great ideas for which that word historically stands.

The Protestant Catholic Church shall be the spring and energy of science and art and of all education. The University shall at last arise. Sown in the days of Alcuin and Abelard, the chivalry of science and art shall come to its flower. The disclosure of the free and democratic constitution of the great mediæval universities of Oxford, Paris and Bologna comes as a surprise to those whose ideas of a university have been formed on the model of Harvard and Yale, and the like prim high schools and knowledge shops of modern Europe. But the mediæval schools, like the modern, were stifled in Aristotle and doted on dead things; the University is in the future, awaiting the rise of a democratic catholicism.

The soul of the University is the passion for the Eternal. It risks its life continually upon the reality of the ideal. It does not principally exist to teach—everything else in the world exists to teach; the University exists to discover and to create. It seizes upon the eternal ele-

The Religion of Democracy.

ments of things and transmutes them into art and history. It summons the youth and faith of the nations to the infinite and arduous labor of the Revolution. It requires of its children the most perfect purity and self-denial. For no one whose soul is knotted with lust or fear, no prurient glory-seeker, no trap-setter to catch distinction, no one afraid to die in his working clothes as a common man, can be an artist, a man of science and a civilizer.

IV.—The name of the hour is Opportunity. The real office of prophets is to see that the thing come true. The hearts of the people everywhere are aglow with expectation for the coming of justice and beauty upon the earth; but what of that? It is not by expectation that the Idea becomes a Fact—this miracle is wrought by faith. It is by faith that a man gives body to a shadow, and existence to that which otherwise would not have been.

It is not yet settled what kind of a century this new era shall be—God, I think, has not decided, and will not decide. It is not decided whether the City of the Soul shall rise now, or after a while. God was always ready and waiting. He has waited a long time.

There is no Destiny—there is only Opportu-

The Religion of Democracy.

nity and an infinite waiting for the coming of the poets and the artists who shall rejoice in Life on any terms, hearing the singing in the heart of God and sending back a brave antiphonal across all the deserts and wildernesses of the world.

THE END.

www.ingramcontent.com/pod-product-compliance
Lightning Source LLC
Chambersburg PA
CBHW030306170426
43202CB00009B/884